Devotionals with

Laura

Laura Ingalls' Favorite Bible Selections

What They Meant in Her Life

What They Might Mean in Yours

Dan L. White

Walnut Grove, Minnesota

The author and his wife Margie and five children settled in the Ozarks some years ago on a forty acre farmstead about twelve miles up the road from Laura's Rocky Ridge Farm.

Published by Ashley Preston Publishing
Hartville, Mo. 65667

www.danlwhitebooks.com

Cover by Carrie A. White Gaffney

Little House is a registered trademark of HarperCollins Publishers Inc.

ISBN 13: 978-1441432612
ISBN 10: 1441432612

Also available in electronic format.

Table of Contents

Prologue   5

Chapter One   21
In facing a crisis, read 46 Psalm

Chapter Two   33
When discouraged, 23 and 24

Chapter Three   51
Lonely or fearful, 27

Chapter Four   65
Planning budget, St. Luke chapter 19

Chapter Five   77
To live successfully with others, read Romans chapter 12

Chapter Six   89
Sick or in pain, read 91 Psalm

Chapter Seven   103
When you travel carry with you 121 Psalm

Chapter Eight   111
*When very weary read Matthew 11:28 & 30 and
Romans 8:31 to 39*

Chapter Nine   121
When things are going from bad to worse 2 Timothy 3d

Chapter Ten   131
When friends go back on you hold to I Corinthians 13th

Chapter Eleven   141
For inward peace the 14th chapter of St. John

Chapter Twelve   153
To avoid misfortune Matthew 7:24 to 27

Chapter Thirteen   161
For record for what trust in God can do Hebrews 11

Chapter Fourteen   173
If you are having to put up a fight, the end of Ephesians

Chapter Fifteen   181
When you have sinned read I John 3:1 – 21

Chapter Sixteen   191
And make Psalm 51 your prayer

Other Books by Dan L. White   201

Devotionals with Laura

By Dan L. White

Prologue

In this book, *Devotionals with Laura*, we carefully examine how her favored Bible passages might have helped her at certain times in her life. If you are reading this book, we will make two assumptions. First, we will assume that you are familiar with Laura Ingalls Wilder and her Little House books. (Little House is a registered trademark of Harper Collins Publishers.) Second, we assume that you are familiar with the Bible. (Bible is a public domain collection of books, written by God, available for use by anyone.)

Many people, including our family, first became aware of the Little House books from watching The *Little House on the Prairie* television series. That show was related to Laura's books in the title of the show and names of characters and places, but that's all. There is almost no correlation between those stories and Laura's stories.

Laura Ingalls Wilder wrote eight books; nine, if we include *The First Four Years*, an unfinished manuscript which was found after her death, but was not a finished book. Those books basically tell the story of her life until she was about twenty-two years old. One book, *Farmer Boy*, tells the story of her husband Almanzo's boyhood. There are some variances between her actual life history and the stories, but for the most part those books are her early life, covering the period from about 1868 until 1888.

They are much more than just historical novels, though. They are works of art. Open any one of her eight books at any place, begin reading, and you will then find it hard to stop. People just love her books. I do. You do. After World War II, when the Germans and Japanese had fought so bitterly against us, the US government had Laura's Little House books translated into German and Japanese, because the books gave such a favorable impression of America. The Germans and Japanese have been our allies ever since!

Pa Ingalls moved his family many times, even more than is recorded in the Little House books. That certainly makes for interesting reading, going from Wisconsin to Kansas to Minnesota to South Dakota, but actually living through all those moves might have been a little trying. Finally they stopped moving at De Smet, Dakota Territory, which became South Dakota. There Laura married Almanzo Wilder, whom she called Manly. He had two 160 acre homestead claims when they got married, but due to drought and other misfortune was not able to hold on to either of them. He and Laura both became seriously ill with diphtheria, which permanently affected Manly.

He and another young man had risked driving far out on the prairie during the long, hard winter of 1880-81 to find wheat for the starving town of De Smet, but after his illness, Manly had no tolerance whatever for cold weather. For a while after his illness, Laura and Manly lived with his parents in Minnesota, where they had moved from New York. Then Manly and Laura moved to Florida for about a year. She didn't like the heat and humidity there any better than he liked the cold up north, so they moved back to De Smet.

In 1894 they learned of some railroad advertising billing the Missouri Ozarks as The Land of the Big Red Apple. The railroad had recently come through the area and wanted farmers to grow crops to ship on their new line. Southern Missouri is a lot warmer than South Dakota and not as sultry as Florida, so the Wilders moved there by covered wagon in 1894.

They fit.

They bought forty acres near Mansfield, Missouri, named it Rocky Ridge, and never gave it up. Their life there was far from easy, but they loved it. Their white clapboard, rambling farmhouse is still there, and is now a part of a museum. Thousands of Little House readers tour it every year.

Their only living child, daughter Rose Wilder Lane, became a nationally known writer early in the twentieth century. In 1911 Laura began to write articles for a farm magazine, the *Missouri Ruralist*. She did that up until the mid 1920's. Her first book was published in 1932, when she was 65 years old. Her last book was published in 1943, when she was 76. All her books were immediately popular.

Manly died in 1949 at the age of 92. Laura followed in 1957, at the age of 90. She has been gone for better than half a century, and it has been longer than that since her books first appeared, during the Great Depression and the Second World War. They are still extremely well liked, very widely read, and have become classics in American literature.

In the house at Rocky Ridge is a rocker where Laura rested and read. After her death, Laura's small Bible was found by the rocker. Inside that Bible were some handwritten notes, listing Laura's favorite Bible selections. Here is what they said.

- In facing a crisis read 46 Psalm
- When discouraged 23 & 24
- Lonely or fearful 27
- Planning budget St. Luke chapter 19
- To live successfully with others read Romans chapter 12

- Sick or in pain read 91 Psalm
- When you travel carry with you 121 Psalm
- When very weary read Matthew 11:28 & 30 and Romans 8:31 to 39
- When things are going from bad to worse 2 Timothy 3d
- When friends go back on you hold to I Corinthians 13th
- For inward peace the 14th chapter of St. John
- To avoid misfortune Matthew 7:24 to 27
- For record for what trust in God can do Hebrews 11
- If you are having to put up a fight -- the end of Ephesians
- When you have sinned read I John 3:1 to 21
- And make Psalm 51 your prayer.

Those eighteen sections of the Bible were marked by Laura as being especially valuable. The fact that she did that tells us a lot about her.

What does it tell us?

It tells us that she loved the Bible and placed great value in its teachings. When she marked these eighteen passages, she did not do it for someone else's eyes. These selections were solely for her benefit, for her life and her spiritual needs. At times of distress, despair, or determination, she turned to the Bible, to these passages.

We also know that she knew the Bible well. Her selections are not just from the Psalms or the Gospels, as a Bible dabbler might choose. They go from the middle of the Old Testament all the way to the book of Hebrews, near the end of the New Testament.

Laura's magazine articles were about day by day concerns of a small farm wife and not at all meant as Bible lessons. Yet sometimes they were like Bible lessons, with a verse thrown into the middle of the article. Here are some examples of verses she used, to encourage the qualities these verses teach.

> I Timothy 6:10 – For the love of money is the root of all evil: which while some coveted after, they have erred from the faith, and pierced themselves through with many sorrows.

> Matthew 9:17 – Neither do men put new wine into old bottles: else the bottles break, and the wine runneth out, and the bottles perish: but they put new wine into new bottles, and both are preserved.

> Matthew 7:12 – Therefore all things whatsoever ye would that men should do to you, do ye even so to them: for this is the law and the prophets.

> Luke 17:21 – Neither shall they say, Lo here! Or, lo there! For, behold, the kingdom of God is within you.

> Proverbs 15:1 – A soft answer turneth away wrath: but grievous words stir up anger.

> Proverbs 22:6 – Train up a child in the way he should go: and when he is old, he will not depart from it.

> Zechariah 4:10 – For who hath despised the day of small things? for they shall rejoice, and shall see the plummet in the hand of Zerubbabel *with* those seven; they *are* the eyes of the LORD, which run to and fro through the whole earth.

> Matthew 5:45 - That ye may be the children of your Father which is in heaven: for he maketh his sun to rise on the evil and on the good, and sendeth rain on the just and on the unjust.

Quite a variety there.

These verses were not the main subjects of her articles. A preacher might look up a verse and then make that the subject of his talk, and thus wind up with a less familiar text. Laura did not do that. These verses were off the top of her head, as she threw them in to add to the subject she was writing about. Obviously, in order to just toss them in amidst all different types of subjects, she had to have an extensive knowledge of the Bible.

She said, "Always my mind had a trick of picking a text here and a text there and connecting them together in meaning." When she was writing articles, her topic would call to her mind something God had said in the Bible and she added it in. To do that, though, her head had to be filled to the brim with those words from Him.

Laura wasn't real churchy. She attended regularly, but sometimes she thought that churches and the people in them were a bit hypocritical, as she discussed somewhat in her novels. But Laura was Biblicy. She loved it. She learned it. To whatever degree, she tried to live it. Laura's list of Bible passages tells a mountain about her life values. I will venture to say that most Christians have not taken the time to make a list of their Bible treasures. Perhaps they are not familiar enough with the Bible to even compile such a list. Or they have not cared enough about the Bible to search it out that carefully.

Laura did.

How much time did that take?

The King James Bible has over three quarter of a million words. A computer counted exactly 788,280 words, and then asked for a break.

How did Laura compile a list of favorite selections?

She had to be familiar with the whole Bible to know which parts were her favorites.

How did she know the whole Bible?

By reading and reading and reading. And contemplating and cogitating, meditating and ruminating, and just plain thinking about it, even when she wasn't reading. Like an address book full of friends or a family Bible page full of relatives, this list of Bible verses shows Laura's heart.

It is fascinating to consider the selections that she cherished, to think about her thinking about them, and to muse on what events in her life made her embrace each passage. It is not enough for us just to say that she referred to such and such verses in the Bible. That does not capture what they meant to her.

What did they mean to her?

What do they mean to us?

What is God saying?

In this book we examine those questions.

This is a Bible study book, a devotional. It is for people who are devoted to God, and who study the Bible with devotion. That is our purpose in this work. We do not seek to lift up Laura Ingalls Wilder – not that she would want that. We seek to encourage deep, personal, prolonged reflection on the passages for which she obviously did the same.

This is our format in *Devotionals with Laura*, where we examine her most cherished Bible selections.

First, we give the passage in the King James Version (KJ).

Then we consider what the passage might have meant to Laura and how it might have played a role in her life.

Third, we discuss the passage itself and what it means to us in our lives.

Last, we give the passage in a modern translation, usually the World English Bible (WEB) for the Old Testament and the English Standard Version (ESV) for the New Testament.

I have read and studied the Bible steadily and pretty much daily for over forty years. Even so, I found this study very enjoyable and inspiring. We have lived on forty acres in the Ozarks for more than two decades, only a dozen miles from Laura's Rocky Ridge Farm. We know what it's like to live here. We know the people, the climate, and to some degree what Laura and Manly faced as they tried to cultivate a living from the thin, rocky soil.

When Laura said that she read a certain passage at a time of crisis or discouragement in her life, we reflected on what events might have caused her to do that. When was she in a crisis or when was she discouraged? We closely examined the selection she mentioned to see what it was she was drawing from the Bible there. Then we contemplated what the passage meant to us. Most of all, we reflected on what God is telling those who are trying to follow Him. Again, this is not tidwinkling theology. This is devotion and dedication.

Of course, I had read these selected passages numerous times before. But when I had to look at them in the light of what Laura said they meant to her, and then carefully scrutinize them to see what they meant to me, it brought a new depth of reflection.

In that sense, these are devotionals with Laura. She looked at a passage at a certain time in her life and said 'this means this to me.' We look at that same passage and consider what she said.

We also include comments from her writings which may relate to the passage. And we consider how the words relate to our lives, as she related them to hers.

Devotionals with Laura.

Now –

Given that Laura spent much time over many years reading and reflecting on the Bible, what difference did that make in her life?

How much time did she spend reading her little Bible?

Obviously, from the way she threw verses out of her head and held them close to her soul, she spent a lot of her life reading and reflecting on the Word of God.

Let's say that she spent half an hour a day doing that. Some people are content with a ten minute devotion. Unless you are a speed reader and a hyper-meditator, ten minutes is just a mini-devotional. A devotionette. Hardly time to get your mind off whatever it was on.

So if Laura spent a half hour a day on Bible reading, or rounded down to three hours per week, that's about 150 hours per year. From age 15 to age 65, when Laura published her first book, is 50 years of Bible reading. 50 years times 150 hours per year equals 7,500 hours of Bible reading. If we divide that by a 40 hour work week, Laura would have spent 187 work weeks reading the Bible. That's well over three years worth of work weeks poring over and pouring in God's word.

Would Laura have spent that much time doing that?

I think so. I know many people who consider a half hour a day the very minimum Bible study time. The Bible is a big book. But it comes from a BIG God. It's worth it.

People who don't walk closely with God and don't delight in Him and His word consider such reading a waste of precious time; or at least a bit boring and toilsome. You see, a willing Bible reader doesn't do it out of duty. He does it out of delight. He doesn't have to force himself to pick the Bible up. He has to force himself to put it down. He knows those are not the words of legend. Those are the words of life.

When Laura faced a crisis, she did not force herself to read Psalm 46. She eagerly sought it out. When she was discouraged, she didn't say, "Oh, weariness – now I have to read Psalm 24!" Not at all. Her downtrodden spirit yearned for the words, "Lift up your heads, O ye gates; and be ye lift up, ye everlasting doors; and the King of glory shall come in."

Again –

Given that Laura spent so much time over many years reading and reflecting on the Bible, what difference did that make in her life?

It made this difference.

The spirit of the Little House books came from Laura's little Bible.

How is this so?

1. In the Little House books, the Ingalls had a family based upon Bible principles. Ma and Pa Ingalls loved their children, raised them carefully and the children loved and honored their parents, according to the commandment.

> Eph 6:1-4 ESV
> (1) Children, obey your parents in the Lord, for this is right.
> (2) "Honor your father and mother" (this is the first commandment with a promise),

(3) "that it may go well with you and that you may live long in the land."
(4) Fathers, do not provoke your children to anger, but bring them up in the discipline and instruction of the Lord.

In reality we may be sure that the Ingalls family fell far short of having a perfect family, as we all do. However, when Laura pictured the family in her books, she held them up to a high ideal, that ideal being a Godly, Biblical family.

2. Laura's books are filled with peace. We live in a world today where liberals talk love and love violence. Liberals control the television media, and it is just overflowing with every possible violence the Godless mind can think up, picturing it in the goriest ways possible. Laura's books have no violence. She doesn't have to have killings and fights to hold our attention. Think about it -- the biggest battle in the whole Little House series is a school girl disagreement between Laura and Nellie Oleson.

> Isa 26:3 ESV
> (3) You keep him in perfect peace whose mind is stayed on you, because he trusts in you.

> Isa 32:17-18 ESV
> (17) And the effect of righteousness will be peace, and the result of righteousness, quietness and trust forever.
> (18) My people will abide in a peaceful habitation, in secure dwellings, and in quiet resting places.

Laura's stories stroll quietly down the paths of peace, because that's what her spirit had absorbed. In her magazine articles, she often discussed the need of having peace among people, and in her books, that's how she wrote the stories.

3. The Little House books are filled with a love for God's creation.

We all remember from the books how Laura and her sister Mary took walks on the prairie. First of all, how many writers can hold your interest by describing two girls walking on the prairie? Laura did, and her description of those strolls in the grasses and wildflowers were vivid a half century later. They were vivid because Laura had loved what she was seeing at the time, and the memory and love of God's handiwork had glowed itself into her lifetime memory.

This is a well known quote of hers from a magazine article she wrote.

> *What a beautiful world this is! Have you noticed the wonderful coloring of the sky at sunrise? For me there is no time like the early morning, when the spirit of light broods over the earth at its awakening. What glorious colors in the woods these days! Did you even think that great painters have spent their lives trying to reproduce on canvas what we may see every day?*
>
> *Thousands of dollars are paid for their pictures which are not so beautiful as those nature gives us freely. The colors in the sky at sunset, the delicate mists of the early spring foliage, the brilliant autumn leaves, the softly-colored grasses and lovely flowers – what painter ever equaled their beauties with paint and brush?*
>
> *Psa 8:3-5 KJ*
> *(3) When I consider thy heavens, the work of thy fingers, the moon and the stars, which thou hast ordained;*
> *(4) What is man, that thou art mindful of him? and the son of man, that thou visitest him?*
> *(5) For thou hast made him a little lower than the angels, and hast crowned him with glory and honour.*

I strolled today down a woodland path—
A crow cawed loudly and flew away.
The sky was blue and the clouds were gold
And drifted before me fold on fold;
The leaves were yellow and red and brown
And patter, patter the nuts fell down,
On this beautiful, golden autumn day.
A squirrel was storing his winter hoard,
The world was pleasant: I lingered long,
The brown quails rose with a sudden whirr
And a little bundle, of eyes and fur,
Took shape of a rabbit and leaped away.
A little chipmunk came out to play
And the autumn breeze sang a wonder song.

Laura Ingalls Wilder

That is an open adoration of God through a love of His creation, appreciating that He is creator. She showed that by the verse she quoted. She wasn't just a nature lover. She loved *God's* creation.

The stories of the Little House books came from Laura's life but the spirit of the books came from Laura's little Bible.

Galatians 5:22 lists the fruits of God's spirit.

> Gal 5:22-23 KJ
> (22) But the fruit of the Spirit is love, joy, peace, longsuffering, gentleness, goodness, faith,
> (23) Meekness, temperance: against such there is no law.

Look at what Christ said, which applies to Laura's writing.

> Luk 6:43-45 ESV
> (43) "For no good tree bears bad fruit, nor again does a

bad tree bear good fruit,

(44) for each tree is known by its own fruit. For figs are not gathered from thorn bushes, nor are grapes picked from a bramble bush.

(45) The good person out of the good treasure of his heart produces good, and the evil person out of his evil treasure produces evil, for out of the abundance of the heart his mouth speaks.

He said you don't get figs from a sticker bush. Laura's figs came from the Bible bush. Christ said, "out of the abundance of the heart the mouth speaks." Or in her case, the pencil spoke. All those years of taking in the spirit of the Bible came out in an uplifting, edifying, good spirit in the Little House books.

The fruits of the spirit are –

- Love;
- Joy;
- Peace;
- Longsuffering;
- Gentleness;
- Goodness;
- Faith;
- Meekness;
- Temperance.

Now which one of those did Laura not put in her books?

She put those fruits in her mind and spirit by reading her Bible all those years. When the time came, those fruits budded forth in her books.

In this book we are doing devotionals with Laura. We do not seek to uplift Laura, not that she would want that. In this book we seek to lift up the Father and the Son. We do want to reflect with her and see what the years of Bible reading taught her. We want to repose with those beautiful words in the holy Bible that she loved, and see what God teaches us there.

This is not meant to be a quick read. This is a book of inaction. Don't read more than one chapter a day. Read. Reflect. Pore over His words. Pour in His attitude. Let God's words refine your spirit, slowly, as it must be. May your own house come to be a Little House, filled with peace and gaiety, and may your family frolic together with the fruits of the spirit.

Chapter One

In facing a crisis, read 46 Psalm

Psalm 46

Psa 46:1-11, KJ

(1) God is our refuge and strength, a very present help in trouble.

(2) Therefore will not we fear, though the earth be removed, and though the mountains be carried into the midst of the sea;

(3) Though the waters thereof roar and be troubled, though the mountains shake with the swelling thereof. Selah.

(4) There is a river, the streams whereof shall make glad the city of God, the holy place of the tabernacles of the most High.

(5) God is in the midst of her; she shall not be moved: God shall help her, and that right early.

(6) The heathen raged, the kingdoms were moved: he uttered his voice, the earth melted.

(7) The LORD of hosts is with us; the God of Jacob is our refuge. Selah.

(8) Come, behold the works of the LORD, what desolations he hath made in the earth.

(9) He maketh wars to cease unto the end of the earth; he breaketh the bow, and cutteth the spear in sunder; he burneth the chariot in the fire.

(10) Be still, and know that I am God: I will be exalted among the heathen, I will be exalted in the earth.

(11) The LORD of hosts is with us; the God of Jacob is our refuge. Selah.

Sometimes the crises that people face are widespread, such as the world wars. Verse 9 says that God makes wars to cease, that He breaks the bow, cuts the spear in two, and burns the chariot. In the eighteenth century, the Age of Reason prevailed. God's revelation was suppressed and human reason was elevated in the search for human perfection. From that point it was said that the human spirit could be changed by education. But humans cannot stop having wars. Since the Age of Reason began, wars have gotten worse, not better. Only God can stop wars, and we look forward to that time when He does.

Laura wrote the following in 1919, shortly after the end of the great worldwide crisis of World War I.

> *A great deal is said and written about natural, national boundaries and learned discussions of racial antagonisms as causes of the restlessness and ill-temper of the nations; and there are investigations and commissions and inquiries to discover what is the matter with the world and to find a remedy...*

> *But the cause of all the unrest and strife is easily found. It is selfishness, nothing else, selfishness deep in the hearts of people. It seems rather impossible that such a small thing as individual selfishness could cause so much trouble, but my selfishness added to your selfishness and that added to the selfishness of our neighbors all over the big, round world is not a small thing...*

> *There is no oppression of a group of people but has its root and inception in the hearts of the oppressors. There is no wild lawlessness and riot and bloodlust of a mob but has its place in the hearts of the persons who are that mob. Just so, if justice and fairness and kindness fill the minds of a crowd of persons, those things will be shown in their actions.*

So, if we are eager to help in putting the world to rights, our first duty is to put ourselves right, to overcome our selfishness and be as eager that others shall be treated fairly as we are that no advantage shall be taken of ourselves; and to deal justly and have a loving charity and mercy for others as we wish them to have for us.

Laura Ingalls Wilder

During a great crisis such as a war, people turn back to God. There are no atheists in foxholes.

Most of the crises that we face as individuals are personal crises. Not a World War, but something that changes our own little world.

Laura and Manly had a crisis that touched the lives of many people, including yours. That crisis made a little change in the whole big world. When Laura and Manly came to Mansfield, they had a hundred dollars which they used to paid down on their Rocky Ridge farm. This left them owing mortgage of $200 according to what Laura said in a later article. At first they sold wood to earn money to live on. Rose recalled that the very first cord that Manly sold only brought fifty cents. The usual price was a dollar a cord, a stack four feet tall by four feet deep by eight feet long.

After several years they developed their farm enough so they were able to sell apples, poultry and eggs, and cream. The cabin on Rocky Ridge was a rough log cabin. After a few years living in the rough cabin the Wilders moved into Mansfield and rented a small house. Manly still worked on the farm and at other jobs. Laura cooked meals for railroad workers.

During this time Laura and Manly were at least staying even economically, but were not getting much ahead. They could not get a big house built on their farm, and they were not living at their beloved Rocky Ridge.

Manly's parents had moved from New York state, the site of the book *Farmer Boy*, to Minnesota. They were prosperous farmers there. Laura and Manly had lived with them for a year in Minnesota while Manly recuperated after having diphtheria. Manly's parents eventually visited him and Laura, and as a gift bought them the house they were renting in Mansfield. Laura and Manly sold that house in town and were then able to get their farmhouse built on Rocky Ridge in 1912.

It was 18 years after they moved to the Ozarks before they were able to get their house built on their farm. Rose was long gone, married and far away in California. Manly was 55 years old when the house was finished and he was finally back on his farm full time.

In 1911 Laura was able to begin bringing in a little extra income by writing a regular column about farm life for the *Missouri Ruralist*. Laura also worked for the Farm Loan Association, again to bring in extra income.

They were successful enough financially to expand their original 40 acres to 200, a fair sized farm for the hilly Ozarks. However, when Laura visited Rose in San Francisco in 1915, Rose was trying to convince her parents to move to California, where their farm labors might be easier. Laura did look California over with that in mind, but concluded that she wouldn't trade all of California for one Ozark hill.

In the 1920's Rose, divorced and single, lived with them at Rocky Ridge and was very successful with her writing. The stock market was skyrocketing and Rose invested her good earnings in the market. Toward the end of the 1920's, Laura no longer worked for the Farm Loan Association and no longer wrote columns for the *Missouri Ruralist*. Manly was in his 70's and most of the farm work was taken care of by a hired man.

Laura and Manly were comfortable, had some savings to live on, and were slowing down as they entered the last stage of their lives.

And Rose talked them into investing their money with her broker in the stock market.

In 1929, that money was gone.

That was a crisis.

Young people can take on a crisis. Old people want to take it easy.

In his twenties, thirties, forties and fifties, Manly had fought with farms. He had had a bad leg and a good spirit. But in his seventies, he had a bad leg and an old body. His spirit might still have been willing to wage the war against the rocks and pests and weather, but his flesh was seventy-ish.

When they were ready to settle back, they had to step it up again, just to stay alive.

One of Laura's friends recalls Laura mentioning something referring to that period.

> *Editor: Did Laura talk about their life on the farm much?*
>
> *Nava: She did mention that one time they had a young colt they liked very much. Both Laura and Almanzo liked horses and they had some good stock. But one time -- I think it was in the early thirties -- they had to sell that colt just to pay the taxes on their property. Laura was really sad about having to part with that colt.*
>
> *From our book Laura Ingalls' Friends Remember Her.*

Losing their savings was a crisis that could be with them for the rest of their lives. Surely during that time, when the whole country was suffering, Laura read, "God is our refuge and strength, a very present help in trouble."

Then Laura tried writing again. Not columns, but books. They could use the money.

About 1930, as the depression was really pressing in, Laura asked Rose to help with a book Laura had written. The book was *Pioneer Girl*, the story of Laura's life. The publishers refused the book.

Laura rewrote the story, Rose helped edit it, and in 1932 *Little House in the Big Woods* was published. Laura was 65 years old and had her first successful novel.

The first royalty check was for $500. Wages were about $15 per week, but a quarter of the country was jobless, with no wages. That one check, the smallest she ever received, was the better part of a year's income, if a person had a year's income.

The crisis was past.

That crisis made a little change in the whole big world. The Little House books are read all across America and in many other countries and languages. Laura might have written them even without the financial crisis, but there is no doubt it gave her extra motivation. And surely Psalm 46 gave her extra inspiration.

Psalm 46 speaks of a river in the city of God. Many major cities are built on a river. Jerusalem was not built on a river at all. Jerusalem is on a hill. Rivers don't run on hills. Jerusalem only had a small flow through it.

From Geneva Bible

Psa 46:4 [There is] a *river, the streams whereof shall make glad the city of God, the holy [place] of the tabernacles of the most High.

* The river of Shiloh, which passed through Jerusalem: meaning, though the defense seems small, yet if God has appointed it, it is sufficient.

Isaiah mentioned this small flow.

Isa 8:6-8 WEB
(6) "Because this people have refused the waters of Shiloah that go softly, and rejoice in Rezin and Remaliah's son;
(7) now therefore, behold, the Lord brings upon them the mighty flood waters of the River: the king of Assyria and all his glory. It will come up over all its channels, and go over all its banks.

Hezekiah channeled these waters into Hezekiah's tunnel, which winds up in the Pool of Siloam. This small flow has been there for as long as we know, and it flows there today. Christ was at the Pool of Siloam.

Joh 9:6-7 WEB
(6) When he [Christ] had said this, he spat on the ground, made mud with the saliva, anointed the blind man's eyes with the mud,
(7) and said to him, "Go, wash in the pool of Siloam" (which means "Sent"). So he went away, washed, and came back seeing.

Eventually the city of God will have a living river. Jerusalem will become a river city.

Zec 14:8 WEB
(8) It will happen in that day, that living waters will go out from Jerusalem; half of them toward the eastern sea, and half of them toward the western sea; in summer and in winter will it be.

Rev 22:1 WEB
(1) He showed me a river of water of life, clear as crystal, proceeding out of the throne of God and of the Lamb,

It is natural for us to fear. When we fear, it is also natural for us to rely on ourselves to save ourselves. This is all natural, but it is not Godly.

In life, the greatest idolatry we must overcome is loving ourselves more than we love God.

We can practice this idolatry every day when we spend almost all our waking time focusing on our own personal interests, giving God only a short devotional, if anything at all.

We can practice this idolatry when things go well, and we take the credit for that. We go on as if we succeeded because of our ability and effort. We treat God as the nine lepers treated Christ. He healed them and they gave no thanks.

Most of all, we can practice this idolatry when we inevitably hit a crisis, and in that crisis the power we look to for saving ourselves is ourselves.

At some point, though, we hit such a severe crisis that we realize that overcoming it is beyond our power. We cannot save ourselves. At that point, we have to leave it "in God's hands." What a fearful statement that is – "It's in God's hands now!" When in fact, whose hands are better to hold us in a crisis?

A first principle of life is that God should never be the last resort.

He is to be our refuge or shelter, near to us, so that we never fear. If God is to be near to us in a time of crisis, then we must be near to Him in times of comfort. If He is to be with us in the storm, we must be with Him in the calm. Christ will always be by our side, if we are always at His feet.

Just as the little stream flow of Shiloah in Jerusalem will eventually be overshadowed by a flowing river of living waters, so the faith of God should increase in believers from a little stream to a big river. Crises help us learn that.

> Psa 46:1-11, WEB
> (1) God is our refuge and strength, a very present help in trouble.
> (2) Therefore we won't be afraid, though the earth changes, though the mountains are shaken into the heart of the seas;
> (3) though its waters roar and are troubled, though the mountains tremble with their swelling. Selah.
> (4) There is a river, the streams of which make the city of God glad, the holy place of the tents of the Most High.
> (5) God is in her midst. She shall not be moved. God will help her at dawn.
> (6) The nations raged. The kingdoms were moved. He lifted his voice, and the earth melted.
> (7) Yahweh of Armies is with us. The God of Jacob is our refuge. Selah.
> (8) Come, see Yahweh's works, what desolations he has made in the earth.
> (9) He makes wars cease to the end of the earth. He breaks the bow, and shatters the spear. He burns the chariots in the fire.

(10) Be still, and know that I am God. I will be exalted among the nations. I will be exalted in the earth.
(11) Yahweh of Armies is with us. The God of Jacob is our refuge. Selah.

Chapter Two

When discouraged, 23 and 24

Psalm 23

Psa 23:1-6 KJ
A psalm of David.
(1) The LORD is my shepherd; I shall not want.
(2) He maketh me to lie down in green pastures: he leadeth me beside the still waters.
(3) He restoreth my soul: he leadeth me in the paths of righteousness for his name's sake.
(4) Yea, though I walk through the valley of the shadow of death, I will fear no evil: for thou art with me; thy rod and thy staff they comfort me.
(5) Thou preparest a table before me in the presence of mine enemies: thou anointest my head with oil; my cup runneth over.
(6) Surely goodness and mercy shall follow me all the days of my life: and I will dwell in the house of the LORD for ever.

Psalm 23 appears in *The Long Winter*, as the teacher starts school with it.

"The school will come to attention," she said. She opened her Bible. "This morning I will read the twenty-third Psalm."

Laura knew the Psalms by heart, of course, but she loved to hear again every word of the twenty-third, from "The Lord is my shepherd: I shall not want,' " to

"Surely goodness and mercy shall follow me all the days of my life: and I will dwell in the house of the Lord forever."

Then Teacher closed the Bible and on all the desks the pupils opened their textbooks. School work had begun."

Notice that "Laura knew the Psalms by heart, of course, but she loved to hear again every word of the twenty-third."

There are 150 psalms.

This psalm is renowned as one of the most beautiful pieces of writing ever recorded. It is brief, yet beautiful, concise and clear, yet charming and captivating. Written by David, a shepherd in his youth, it pictures a shepherd caring for his flock. David knew that well. David cared for his lambs. He was also a lamb who was cared for.

The spirit of God and David's life gave us this sweet song.

> 2Sa 23:1-2: WEB
> David the son of Jesse says, the man who was raised on high says, the anointed of the God of Jacob, *the sweet psalmist of Israel*: The Spirit of Yahweh spoke by me. *His word was on my tongue.*

Never is that truer than in the 23rd Psalm.

In former times in America, many young people memorized this psalm, as Laura did. Such is not the case today. On a nationally televised game show, three very intelligent college students were competing with questions and answers in different subject areas. On most subject areas, they recognized the answers quickly, pushing their buzzers instantly to be able to respond. However, one of the subject areas that these outstanding college students faced was the Bible. In one instance they needed to fill in the missing word from this phrase: "The LORD is my _____."

None of the three brainiacs knew that word. Those extremely well educated young people had no familiarity whatsoever with the 23rd Psalm.

What a tragedy in their personal lives to not have that knowledge.

Even if Psalm 23 is short, there is great depth. The phrases of the song fit in with seven of the ten compound names of Yahweh used in the Bible.

The name Yahweh, the actual personal name of God Almighty, is in the third commandment, although most English translations render it as LORD, which is not a translation of the name itself.

> Exo 20:7 WEB
> (7) "You shall not take the name of Yahweh your God in vain, for Yahweh will not hold him guiltless who takes his name in vain.

Counting the deletions of the scribes, the name Yahweh occurs about 7,000 times in the Hebrew Scriptures, the Old Testament. In the Greek scriptures, the New Testament, the Messiah's original name is Yahweh's Salvation, Y'shua. The name Yahweh itself is like the verb "to be," or existence. Without Him, nothing is.

Notice how the 23rd Psalm connects with these seven compound names of Yahweh. (Quotes from WEB.)

1. Yahweh is my shepherd: Yahweh Roi, shepherd.

> Ps 23:1, only here.

2. I shall lack nothing. Yahweh Yireh, provider.

> Gen 22:12-14
> (12) He said, "Don't lay your hand on the boy, neither do anything to him. For now I know that you fear God, seeing you have not withheld your son, your only son, from me."
> (13) Abraham lifted up his eyes, and looked, and saw that behind him was a ram caught in the thicket by his horns. Abraham went and took the ram, and offered him up for a burnt offering instead of his son.
> (14) Abraham called the name of that place Yahweh Will Provide. As it is said to this day, "On Yahweh's mountain, it will be provided."

3. He leads me beside still waters. Waters of rest, Yahweh Shalom, peace giver.

> Jdg 6:22-24
> (22) Gideon saw that he was the angel of Yahweh; and Gideon said, Alas, Lord Yahweh! because I have seen the angel of Yahweh face to face.
> (23) Yahweh said to him, Peace be to you; don't be afraid: you shall not die.
> (24) Then Gideon built an altar there to Yahweh, and called it Yahweh is Peace: to this day it is still in Ophrah of the Abiezrites.

4. He restores my soul. Yahweh Ropheka, healer.

> Exo 15:26
> (26) and he said, "If you will diligently listen to the voice of Yahweh your God, and will do that which is right in his eyes, and will pay attention to his commandments, and keep all his statutes, I will put none of the diseases on you, which I have put on the Egyptians; for I am Yahweh who heals you."

5. He guides me in the paths of righteousness for his name's sake. Yahweh Tsidkenu, righteousness.

> Jer 23:6
> (6) In his days Judah shall be saved, and Israel shall dwell safely; and this is his name by which he shall be called: Yahweh our righteousness.

6. Even though I walk through the valley of the shadow of death, I will fear no evil, for you are with me. Yahweh Shammah, is there, or companion.

> Eze 48:35
> (35) It shall be eighteen thousand reeds around: and the name of the city from that day shall be, Yahweh is there.

7. You anoint my head with oil. Mekaddishkem, to sanctify you.

> Exo 31:13
> (13) "Speak also to the children of Israel, saying, 'Most certainly you shall keep my Sabbaths: for it is a sign between me and you throughout your generations; that you may know that I am Yahweh who sanctifies you.

The 23rd Psalm, connecting with the names of God, shows us that whatever we need, He is. Shepherd, provider, peace giver, healer, righteousness, companion, sanctifier. Whatever we need, He is.

> Psa 23:1-6 WEB
> Yahweh is my shepherd:
> I shall lack nothing.
> He makes me lie down in green pastures.
> He leads me beside still waters.
> He restores my soul.

He guides me in the paths of righteousness for his name's sake.
Even though I walk through the valley of the shadow of death,
I will fear no evil, for you are with me.
Your rod and your staff, they comfort me.
You prepare a table before me in the presence of my enemies.
You anoint my head with oil.
My cup runs over.
Surely goodness and loving kindness shall follow me all the days of my life, and I will dwell in Yahweh's house forever.

Psalm 24

Psa 24:1-10 KJ
A Psalm of David.
(1) The earth is the LORD'S, and the fulness thereof; the world, and they that dwell therein.
(2) For he hath founded it upon the seas, and established it upon the floods.
(3) Who shall ascend into the hill of the LORD? or who shall stand in his holy place?
(4) He that hath clean hands, and a pure heart; who hath not lifted up his soul unto vanity, nor sworn deceitfully.
(5) He shall receive the blessing from the LORD, and righteousness from the God of his salvation.
(6) This is the generation of them that seek him, that seek thy face, O Jacob. Selah.
(7) Lift up your heads, O ye gates; and be ye lift up, ye everlasting doors; and the King of glory shall come in.
(8) Who is this King of glory? The LORD strong and mighty, the LORD mighty in battle.
(9) Lift up your heads, O ye gates; even lift them up, ye everlasting doors; and the King of glory shall come in.
(10) Who is this King of glory? The LORD of hosts, he is the King of glory. Selah.

When we are down-hearted and discouraged, we speak of looking at the world through blue glasses; nothing looks the same to us; our family and friends do not appear the same; our home and work show in the darkest colors. But when we are happy, we see things in a brighter light and everything is transformed.

Laura Ingalls Wilder

Laura certainly had many opportunities to be discouraged in her life. She had a sister who went blind, a baby brother who died, a baby son who died, a house fire, a husband who had a stroke at a young age – et cetera, et cetera, et cetera.

Indeed Laura had many opportunities to be discouraged, if she had been looking for reasons to be so. She was not. Ma and Pa Ingalls had taught her certain sayings, such as "All's well that ends well," and "Don't cry over spilled milk," which discourage discouragement.

When they first moved to the Ozarks, Laura and Manly had a hundred dollars to pay down on a farm. The hundred dollar bill was carried in a lap desk which Manly had built for Laura. She wrote a diary of their trip down on that desk. When they found Rocky Ridge, they could not find their hundred dollar bill. It had slipped into a crack in the side of the little desk.

Again – just one more great opportunity to be discouraged!

They went on. They did not cry over spilled milk. Manly looked for work in town – didn't find any – and they continued camping in the woods west of Mansfield. In a few days the hundred dollar bill was found, doubtless because Laura spent much time looking for it, even prying down into the joint of the desk where the bill had slipped, and Rocky Ridge became their farm.

With all those times in her life when Laura could have been discouraged – what good would that have done? That would have only made bad times worse.

One outstanding quality of her books is that Laura had the vision to see beauty where others saw barrenness. Maybe that was a natural gift, and perhaps she worked at it. Being discouraged did not seem to be a real strong trait of hers.

And reading Psalms 23 and 24 also helped lift up her spirits.

> *As we go about our daily tasks the work will seem lighter if we enjoy these beautiful things that are just outside our doors and windows. It pays to go to the top of the hill now and then to see the view and to stroll thru the woodlot or pasture forgetting that we are in a hurry or that there is such a thing as a clock in the world. You are "so busy!" Oh, yes, I know it! We are all busy, but what are we living for anyway, and why is the world so beautiful if not for us? The habits we form last us through this life, and I firmly believe into the next. Let's not make such a habit of hurry and work that when we leave this world, we will feel impelled to hurry through the spaces of the universe using our wings for feather dusters to clean away the star dust.*

> *Laura Ingalls Wilder*

Psalm 24 asks the question, Who may climb to His hill?

It answers that question, He who has clean hands.

Jewish writers say that this Psalm remembers when David brought the Ark of the Covenant from the house of Obed-edom to the city of Zion. But that brings up how the Ark of the Covenant wound up at the house of Obed-edom.

> 2Sa 6:1-3 WEB
> (1) David again gathered together all the chosen men of Israel, thirty thousand.

(2) David arose, and went with all the people who were with him, from Baale Judah, to bring up from there the ark of God, which is called by the Name, even the name of Yahweh of Armies who sits above the cherubim.

Notice what a big event that was. David gathered 30,000 chosen men of Israel. Now 30,000 is of itself a big crowd, but these were not just any 30,000. These were a special 30,000, the top chosen men of Israel, particularly picked to participate in this very special event, the bringing of the Ark of the Covenant to Jerusalem.

There were also many other Israelites there. All these people had a certain zeal to serve God. They came out to show their love and respect when the ark of God was moved. But good intentions were not good enough if they were not careful enough to obey. Good intentions should result in good works.

(3) They set the ark of God on a new cart, and brought it out of the house of Abinadab that was in the hill: and Uzzah and Ahio, the sons of Abinadab, drove the new cart.

They set the ark of God on a new cart.

Not just an old cart, mind you, but a brand new cart. Surely the new cart was built to show respect to the ark of God.

That had been done before – by the Philistines.

1Sa 6:1-16 WEB
(1) The ark of Yahweh was in the country of the Philistines seven months.
(2) The Philistines called for the priests and the diviners, saying, "What shall we do with the ark of Yahweh? Show us with which we shall send it to its place."

(3) They said, "If you send away the ark of the God of Israel, don't send it empty; but by all means return him a trespass offering: then you shall be healed, and it shall be known to you why his hand is not removed from you."

(4) Then they said, "What shall be the trespass offering which we shall return to him?" They said, "Five golden tumors, and five golden mice, according to the number of the lords of the Philistines; for one plague was on you all, and on your lords.

(5) Therefore you shall make images of your tumors, and images of your mice that mar the land; and you shall give glory to the God of Israel: peradventure he will lighten his hand from off you, and from off your gods, and from off your land.

(6) Why then do you harden your hearts, as the Egyptians and Pharaoh hardened their hearts? When he had worked wonderfully among them, didn't they let the people go, and they departed?

(7) Now therefore take and prepare yourselves a new cart, and two milk cows, on which there has come no yoke; and tie the cows to the cart, and bring their calves home from them;

(8) and take the ark of Yahweh, and lay it on the cart; and put the jewels of gold, which you return him for a trespass offering, in a coffer by its side; and send it away, that it may go.

(9) Behold; if it goes up by the way of its own border to Beth Shemesh, then he has done us this great evil: but if not, then we shall know that it is not his hand that struck us; it was a chance that happened to us."

(10) The men did so, and took two milk cows, and tied them to the cart, and shut up their calves at home;

(11) and they put the ark of Yahweh on the cart, and the coffer with the mice of gold and the images of their tumors.

(12) The cows took the straight way by the way to Beth Shemesh; they went along the highway, lowing as they went, and didn't turn aside to the right hand or to the left; and the lords of the Philistines went after them to the border of Beth Shemesh.

(13) They of Beth Shemesh were reaping their wheat harvest in the valley; and they lifted up their eyes, and saw the ark, and rejoiced to see it.

(14) The cart came into the field of Joshua of Beth Shemesh, and stood there, where there was a great stone: and they split the wood of the cart, and offered up the cows for a burnt offering to Yahweh.

(15) The Levites took down the ark of Yahweh, and the coffer that was with it, in which the jewels of gold were, and put them on the great stone: and the men of Beth Shemesh offered burnt offerings and sacrificed sacrifices the same day to Yahweh.

(16) When the five lords of the Philistines had seen it, they returned to Ekron the same day.

So the Philistines, who were not worshipers of Yahweh but were Dagon's disciples, had put the Ark of the Covenant on a new cart, and they had lived. Now the people of Israel had followed the example of the Philistines. But Israel was not Philistia. Israel had the word of God and had no business following the example of the heathen.

2 Sam 6:3 - 9

(3) They set the ark of God on a new cart, and brought it out of the house of Abinadab that was in the hill: and Uzzah and Ahio, the sons of Abinadab, drove the new cart.

(4) They brought it out of the house of Abinadab, which was in the hill, with the ark of God: and Ahio went before the ark.

(5) David and all the house of Israel played before Yahweh with all manner of instruments made of fir wood, and with harps, and with stringed instruments, and with tambourines, and with castanets, and with cymbals.
(6) When they came to the threshing floor of Nacon, Uzzah put forth his hand to the ark of God, and took hold of it; for the cattle stumbled.
(7) The anger of Yahweh was kindled against Uzzah; and God struck him there for his error; and there he died by the ark of God.
(8) David was displeased, because Yahweh had broken forth on Uzzah; and he called that place Perez Uzzah, to this day.
(9) David was afraid of Yahweh that day; and he said, How shall the ark of Yahweh come to me?

David asked the question, How shall the ark of Yahweh come to me? Which is like the question in Psalm 24, Who shall climb His hill, to be close to God?

The ark came to David by following the word of Yahweh and not the example of the Philistines.

Num 4:5-15 WEB
(5) When the camp moves forward, Aaron shall go in, and his sons, and they shall take down the veil of the screen, and cover the ark of the Testimony with it,
(6) and shall put a covering of sealskin on it, and shall spread over it a cloth all of blue, and shall put in its poles.
(7) On the table of show bread they shall spread a blue cloth, and put on it the dishes, the spoons, the bowls, and the cups with which to pour out; and the continual bread shall be on it.

(8) They shall spread on them a scarlet cloth, and cover the same with a covering of sealskin, and shall put in its poles.

(9) They shall take a blue cloth, and cover the lampstand of the light, and its lamps, and its snuffers, and its snuff dishes, and all its oil vessels, with which they minister to it.

(10) They shall put it and all its vessels within a covering of sealskin, and shall put it on the frame.

(11) On the golden altar they shall spread a blue cloth, and cover it with a covering of sealskin, and shall put in its poles.

(12) They shall take all the vessels of ministry, with which they minister in the sanctuary, and put them in a blue cloth, and cover them with a covering of sealskin, and shall put them on the frame.

(13) They shall take away the ashes from the altar, and spread a purple cloth on it.

(14) They shall put on it all its vessels, with which they minister about it, the fire pans, the flesh hooks, the shovels, and the basins; all the vessels of the altar; and they shall spread on it a covering of sealskin, and put in its poles.

(15) "When Aaron and his sons have finished covering the sanctuary, and all the furniture of the sanctuary, as the camp moves forward; after that, the sons of Kohath shall come to carry it: but they shall not touch the sanctuary, lest they die. These things are the burden of the sons of Kohath in the Tent of Meeting.

The word of Yahweh did not say to put the ark on a new cart. Human wisdom came up with that idea. God does not care for human wisdom, particularly when it overrules God's wisdom.

David and Israel had to learn to respect the word of God. When David learned that, then he could bring the ark to Jerusalem.

2 Sam 6:10-15 WEB
(10) So David would not remove the ark of Yahweh to him into the city of David; but David carried it aside into the house of Obed-Edom the Gittite.
(11) The ark of Yahweh remained in the house of Obed-Edom the Gittite three months: and Yahweh blessed Obed-Edom, and all his house.
(12) It was told king David, saying, Yahweh has blessed the house of Obed-Edom, and all that pertains to him, because of the ark of God. David went and brought up the ark of God from the house of Obed-Edom into the city of David with joy.
(13) It was so, that, when those who bore the ark of Yahweh had gone six paces, he sacrificed an ox and a fattened calf.
(14) David danced before Yahweh with all his might; and David was girded with a linen ephod.
(15) So David and all the house of Israel brought up the ark of Yahweh with shouting, and with the sound of the trumpet.

David had asked the question, How shall the ark of God come to me? And the answer was, according to the specific instructions of the word of God.

Psalm 24 asks the question, Psa 24:3 WEB
(3) Who may ascend to Yahweh's hill? Who may stand in his holy place?

In the same way, the answer is those who follow God's word.

Psa 24:4-5 WEB
(4) He who has clean hands and a pure heart; who has not lifted up his soul to falsehood, and has not sworn deceitfully.
(5) He shall receive a blessing from Yahweh, righteousness from the God of his salvation.

Those who try hard to follow God in this world will always have trouble because of that. Many are the afflictions of the righteous, Ps 34:19.

Trouble can be discouraging. However, it is encouraging to know that the presence of God will be with those who follow the word of God, who keep clean hands and avoid falsehood. These are not people who build a new cart for the ark and demand that God accept that. These are people who seek God's will – who take the time to look up His instructions -- and are willing to follow that.

For those people – "Lift up your heads, you gates; yes, lift them up, you everlasting doors, and the King of glory will come in."

That's encouraging.

> Psa 24:1-10 WEB
> (1) The earth is Yahweh's, with its fullness; the world, and those who dwell therein.
> (2) For he has founded it on the seas, and established it on the floods.
> (3) Who may ascend to Yahweh's hill? Who may stand in his holy place?
> (4) He who has clean hands and a pure heart; who has not lifted up his soul to falsehood, and has not sworn deceitfully.
> (5) He shall receive a blessing from Yahweh, righteousness from the God of his salvation.
> (6) This is the generation of those who seek Him, who seek your face--even Jacob. Selah.
> (7) Lift up your heads, you gates! Be lifted up, you everlasting doors, and the King of
> glory will come in.
> (8) Who is the King of glory? Yahweh strong and mighty, Yahweh mighty in battle.

(9) Lift up your heads, you gates; yes, lift them up, you everlasting doors, and the King of glory will come in.
(10) Who is this King of glory? Yahweh of Armies is the King of glory! Selah.

Chapter Three

Lonely or fearful, 27

Psalm 27

Psa 27:1-14 KJ
A Psalm of David.
(1) The LORD is my light and my salvation; whom shall I fear? the LORD is the strength of my life; of whom shall I be afraid?
(2) When the wicked, even mine enemies and my foes, came upon me to eat up my flesh, they stumbled and fell.
(3) Though an host should encamp against me, my heart shall not fear: though war should rise against me, in this will I be confident.
(4) One thing have I desired of the LORD, that will I seek after; that I may dwell in the house of the LORD all the days of my life, to behold the beauty of the LORD, and to enquire in his temple.
(5) For in the time of trouble he shall hide me in his pavilion: in the secret of his tabernacle shall he hide me; he shall set me up upon a rock.
(6) And now shall mine head be lifted up above mine enemies round about me: therefore will I offer in his tabernacle sacrifices of joy; I will sing, yea, I will sing praises unto the LORD.
(7) Hear, O LORD, when I cry with my voice: have mercy also upon me, and answer me.
(8) When thou saidst, Seek ye my face; my heart said unto thee, Thy face, LORD, will I seek.

(9) Hide not thy face far from me; put not thy servant away in anger: thou hast been my help; leave me not, neither forsake me, O God of my salvation.

(10) When my father and my mother forsake me, then the LORD will take me up.

(11) Teach me thy way, O LORD, and lead me in a plain path, because of mine enemies.

(12) Deliver me not over unto the will of mine enemies: for false witnesses are risen up against me, and such as breathe out cruelty.

(13) I had fainted, unless I had believed to see the goodness of the LORD in the land of the living.

(14) Wait on the LORD: be of good courage, and he shall strengthen thine heart: wait, I say, on the LORD.

Laura said she read Psalm 27 when she was lonely or fearful. There was a time, for nearly eight years, when Manly was already gone and Laura was alone.

Not long since a friend said to me, "Growing old is the saddest thing in the world." Since then I have been thinking about growing old, trying to decide if I thought her right. But I cannot agree with her. True, we lose some things that we prize as time passes and acquire a few that we would prefer to be without. But we may gain infinitely more with the years than we lose in wisdom, character, and the sweetness of life...

As New Year after New Year comes, these waves upon the river of life bear us farther along toward the ocean of Eternity, either protesting the inevitable and looking longingly back toward years that are gone or with calmness and faith facing the future serene in the knowledge that the power behind life's currents is strong and good.

And thinking of these things, I have concluded that whether it is sad to grow old depends on how we face it, whether we are looking forward with confidence or backward with regret. Still, in any case, it takes courage to live long successfully, and they are brave who grow old with smiling faces.

Laura Ingalls Wilder

I spoke with a good friend of Laura's about the time of Manly's passing. Again, this is from our book *Laura Ingalls' Friends Remember Her*.

Editor: Do you recall when Almanzo passed away?

Neta: Well, Mrs. Wilder called us and told us that he was sick and to come quick. We were getting ready to go to church -- Sunday night -- so we went out there. When we got out there, he was sitting in one of those big, wide-armed chairs, and she was holding him in the chair. I knew he was gone, 'cause you could tell that he was. We called the doctor out and he said, "No, he's gone."

We were satisfied that he was, but she was just a-holding him in that chair.

Editor: She just wouldn't let him go?

Neta: No. So after that, we would call her and talk to her and we were out there all the time. She depended on us a lot.

Editor: While Laura was holding Almanzo, did she know he had gone?

Neta: I think she did, yes. She just didn't want to let him go.

Editor: Did you stay with her that night?

Neta: I don't remember. Rose came in a day or two. There was a friend of Laura's that lived north of town, Mary Pool, and she wanted to stay with her. I think she stayed about two nights after he was buried, and Laura said, "Neta, will you stay at night with me for a while?"

My husband didn't care if I went and stayed with her for a while. So I said, "Yes, I'll stay with you."

She said, "Well, you know what? Mary asked to stay, but she won't go to bed. She sleeps in a chair. I'm not going to let her stay here with me if she won't go to bed."

I don't remember how long I stayed with her until she said, "It's all right. You can go home now."

The bed next to her office was his bed, and hers was next to the bathroom. That night, when we went to go to bed, she said, "Neta, do you care if I sleep in Almanzo's bed and you sleep in mine?"

And I said, "I don't care where I sleep."

I don't know if she felt closer to him sleeping in his bed.

Manly and Laura were married in 1885. He passed in 1949. They were together for 64 years, not counting the courtship time and the buggy rides between the twin lakes at De Smet. With her companion and soul mate of almost seven decades gone, Laura would have been lonely.

Psalm 27 is about not being afraid.

Notice:

- Of whom shall I be afraid?
- ...my heart shall not fear.
- For in the day of trouble he will keep me...
- ...he will hide me.
- Don't abandon me, neither forsake me...

To know this Psalm is to know the heart of David.
This Psalm speaks of finding safety in God.

Just glance over some of David's psalms and this is what we see.

> Psa 3:2-6 WEB
> (2) Many there are who say of my soul, "There is no help for him in God." Selah.
> (3) But you, Yahweh, are a shield around me, my glory, and the one who lifts up my head.
> (4) I cry to Yahweh with my voice, and he answers me out of his holy hill. Selah.
> (5) I laid myself down and slept. I awakened; for Yahweh sustains me.
> (6) I will not be afraid of tens of thousands of people who have set themselves against me on every side.
>
> Psa 4:1-5 WEB
> (1) Answer me when I call, God of my righteousness. Give me relief from my distress. Have mercy on me, and hear my prayer.
> (2) You sons of men, how long shall my glory be turned into dishonor? Will you love vanity, and seek after falsehood? Selah.
> (3) But know that Yahweh has set apart for himself him who is godly: Yahweh will hear when I call to him.
> (4) Stand in awe, and don't sin. Search your own heart on your bed, and be still. Selah.
> (5) Offer the sacrifices of righteousness. Put your trust in Yahweh.

Psa 5:11 WEB
(11) But let all those who take refuge in you rejoice,
Let them always shout for joy, because you defend
them. Let them also who love your name be joyful in
you.

Psa 6:1-4 WEB
(1) Yahweh, don't rebuke me in your anger, neither
discipline me in your wrath.
(2) Have mercy on me, Yahweh, for I am faint.
Yahweh, heal me, for my bones are troubled.
(3) My soul is also in great anguish. But you, Yahweh-
-how long?
(4) Return, Yahweh. Deliver my soul, and save me for
your loving kindness' sake.

Psa 7:1 WEB
(1) Yahweh, my God, I take refuge in you. Save me
from all those who pursue me, and deliver me,

Psa 7:10
(10) My shield is with God, who saves the upright in
heart.

Psa 9:9-10 WEB
(9) Yahweh will also be a high tower for the oppressed;
a high tower in times of trouble.
(10) Those who know your name will put their trust in
you, for you, Yahweh, have not forsaken those who
seek you.

For David, Yahweh God was deliverance. Over and over that is
repeated in the psalms which David wrote, in song after song
which he composed and sang to God. That is what made David,
David. He trusted God.

Because of that deep belief, David was able to do this.

Now the Philistines gathered together their armies to battle; and they were gathered together at Socoh, which belongs to Judah, and encamped between Socoh and Azekah, in Ephesdammim. Saul and the men of Israel were gathered together, and encamped in the valley of Elah, and set the battle in array against the Philistines. The Philistines stood on the mountain on the one side, and Israel stood on the mountain on the other side: and there was a valley between them. There went out a champion out of the camp of the Philistines, named Goliath, of Gath, whose height was six cubits and a span. He had a helmet of brass on his head, and he was clad with a coat of mail; and the weight of the coat was five thousand shekels of brass. He had brass shin armor on his legs, and a javelin of brass between his shoulders. The staff of his spear was like a weaver's beam; and his spear's head weighed six hundred shekels of iron: and his shield bearer went before him.

He stood and cried to the armies of Israel, and said to them, "Why have you come out to set your battle in array? Am I not a Philistine, and you servants to Saul? Choose a man for you, and let him come down to me. If he be able to fight with me, and kill me, then will we be your servants; but if I prevail against him, and kill him, then you will be our servants, and serve us."

The Philistine said, "I defy the armies of Israel this day; give me a man, that we may fight together."

When Saul and all Israel heard those words of the Philistine, they were dismayed, and greatly afraid.

Now David was the son of that Ephrathite of Bethlehem Judah, whose name was Jesse; and he had eight sons: and the man was an old man in the days of Saul, stricken in years among men. The three eldest sons of

Jesse had gone after Saul to the battle: and the names of his three sons who went to the battle were Eliab the firstborn, and next to him Abinadab, and the third Shammah. David was the youngest; and the three eldest followed Saul.

Now David went back and forth from Saul to feed his father's sheep at Bethlehem.

The Philistine drew near morning and evening, and presented himself forty days.

Jesse said to David his son, "Take now for your brothers an ephah of this parched grain, and these ten loaves, and carry them quickly to the camp to your brothers; and bring these ten cheeses to the captain of their thousand, and look how your brothers fare, and take their pledge."

Now Saul, and they, and all the men of Israel, were in the valley of Elah, fighting with the Philistines. David rose up early in the morning, and left the sheep with a keeper, and took, and went, as Jesse had commanded him; and he came to the place of the wagons, as the army which was going forth to the fight shouted for the battle. Israel and the Philistines put the battle in array, army against army.

David left his baggage in the hand of the keeper of the baggage, and ran to the army, and came and greeted his brothers. As he talked with them, behold, there came up the champion, the Philistine of Gath, Goliath by name, out of the ranks of the Philistines, and spoke according to the same words: and David heard them.

All the men of Israel, when they saw the man, fled from him, and were sore afraid.

The men of Israel said, "Have you seen this man who is come up? Surely to defy Israel is he come up. And it shall be, that the man who kills him, the king will enrich him with great riches, and will give him his daughter, and make his father's house free in Israel."

David spoke to the men who stood by him, saying, "What shall be done to the man who kills this Philistine, and takes away the reproach from Israel? For who is this uncircumcised Philistine, that he should defy the armies of the living God?"

The people answered him after this manner, saying, "So shall it be done to the man who kills him."

Eliab his eldest brother heard when he spoke to the men. And Eliab's anger was kindled against David, and he said, "Why have you come down? And with whom have you left those few sheep in the wilderness? I know your pride, and the naughtiness of your heart; for you have come down that you might see the battle."

David said, "What have I now done? Is there not a cause?"

He turned away from him toward another, and spoke after the same manner: and the people answered him again after the former manner.

When the words were heard which David spoke, they rehearsed them before Saul; and he sent for him.

David said to Saul, "Let no man's heart fail because of him; your servant will go and fight with this Philistine."

Saul said to David, "You are not able to go against this Philistine to fight with him; for you are but a youth, and he a man of war from his youth."

David said to Saul, "Your servant was keeping his father's sheep; and when there came a lion, or a bear, and took a lamb out of the flock, I went out after him, and struck him, and delivered it out of his mouth; and when he arose against me, I caught him by his beard, and struck him, and killed him. Your servant struck both the lion and the bear: and this uncircumcised Philistine shall be as one of them, seeing he has defied the armies of the living God."

David said, "Yahweh who delivered me out of the paw of the lion, and out of the paw of the bear, he will deliver me out of the hand of this Philistine."

Saul said to David, "Go, and Yahweh shall be with you."

Saul clad David with his clothing, and he put a helmet of brass on his head, and he clad him with a coat of mail. David girded his sword on his clothing, and he tried to go; for he had not proved it.

David said to Saul, "I can't go with these; for I have not proved them."

David put them off him. He took his staff in his hand, and chose him five smooth stones out of the brook, and put them in the shepherd's bag which he had, even in his wallet; and his sling was in his hand: and he drew near to the Philistine.

The Philistine came on and drew near to David; and the man who bore the shield went before him. When the Philistine looked about, and saw David, he disdained him; for he was but a youth, and ruddy, and withal of a fair face.

The Philistine said to David, "Am I a dog, that you come to me with sticks?"

The Philistine cursed David by his gods. The Philistine said to David, "Come to me, and I will give your flesh to the birds of the sky, and to the animals of the field."

Then said David to the Philistine, "You come to me with a sword, and with a spear, and with a javelin. But I come to you in the name of Yahweh of Armies, the God of the armies of Israel, whom you have defied. This day Yahweh will deliver you into my hand. And I will strike you, and take your head from off you. And I will give the dead bodies of the army of the Philistines this day to the birds of the sky, and to the wild animals of the earth; that all the earth may know that there is a God in Israel, and that all this assembly may know that Yahweh doesn't save with sword and spear. For the battle is Yahweh's, and he will give you into our hand."

It happened, when the Philistine arose, and came and drew near to meet David, that David hurried, and ran toward the army to meet the Philistine. David put his hand in his bag, and took there a stone, and slang it, and struck the Philistine in his forehead; and the stone sank into his forehead, and he fell on his face to the earth.

(1Sa 17:1-49, WEB, with some punctuation changed.)

Notice that David, this young kid whose biggest job had been taking care of lambing ewes, said that God does not save with spear and sword. David went out to meet Goliath with a sling and a stone, but that young man absolutely knew that his salvation did not depend on a skinny slingshot.

Notice that Saul saw nothing but a skinny youth fighting against Goliath. David saw God fighting against Goliath. God said that David was a man after God's own heart. David's heart sought God Himself. In times of trouble, and he had many, David looked to God for His security. More than anything else, that is what made David who he was. He really trusted God.

Heb 11:6 ESV
(6) And without faith it is impossible to please him, for whoever would draw near to God must believe that he exists and that he rewards those who seek him. That is what David did. In all his times of trouble, when he was lonely or fearful, he sought God, and knew that He would be there.

Psa 27:1-14 WEB
(1) Yahweh is my light and my salvation. Whom shall I fear? Yahweh is the strength of my life. Of whom shall I be afraid?
(2) When evildoers came at me to eat up my flesh, even my adversaries and my foes, they stumbled and fell.
(3) Though an army should encamp against me, my heart shall not fear. Though war should rise against me, even then I will be confident.
(4) One thing I have asked of Yahweh, that I will seek after, that I may dwell in the house of Yahweh all the days of my life, to see Yahweh's beauty, and to inquire in his temple.
(5) For in the day of trouble he will keep me secretly in his pavilion. In the covert of his tabernacle he will hide me. He will lift me up on a rock.
(6) Now my head will be lifted up above my enemies around me. I will offer sacrifices of joy in his tent. I will sing, yes, I will sing praises to Yahweh.
(7) Hear, Yahweh, when I cry with my voice. Have mercy also on me, and answer me.
(8) When you said, "Seek my face, "my heart said to you, "I will seek your face, Yahweh."

(9) Don't hide your face from me. Don't put your servant away in anger. You have been my help. Don't abandon me, neither forsake me, God of my salvation.

(10) When my father and my mother forsake me, then Yahweh will take me up.

(11) Teach me your way, Yahweh. Lead me in a straight path, because of my enemies.

(12) Don't deliver me over to the desire of my adversaries, for false witnesses have risen up against me, such as breathe out cruelty.

(13) I am still confident of this: I will see the goodness of Yahweh in the land of the living.

(14) Wait for Yahweh. Be strong, and let your heart take courage. Yes, wait for Yahweh.

Chapter Four

Planning budget, St. Luke chapter 19

Luke 19

Luk 19:11-26 KJ

(11) And as they heard these things, he added and spake a parable, because he was nigh to Jerusalem, and because they thought that the kingdom of God should immediately appear.

(12) He said therefore, A certain nobleman went into a far country to receive for himself a kingdom, and to return.

(13) And he called his ten servants, and delivered them ten pounds, and said unto them, Occupy till I come.

(14) But his citizens hated him, and sent a message after him, saying, We will not have this man to reign over us.

(15) And it came to pass, that when he was returned, having received the kingdom, then he commanded these servants to be called unto him, to whom he had given the money, that he might know how much every man had gained by trading.

(16) Then came the first, saying, Lord, thy pound hath gained ten pounds.

(17) And he said unto him, Well, thou good servant: because thou hast been faithful in a very little, have thou authority over ten cities.

(18) And the second came, saying, Lord, thy pound hath gained five pounds.

(19) And he said likewise to him, Be thou also over five cities.

(20) And another came, saying, Lord, behold, here is thy pound, which I have kept laid up in a napkin:

(21) For I feared thee, because thou art an austere man: thou takest up that thou layedst not down, and reapest that thou didst not sow.

(22) And he saith unto him, Out of thine own mouth will I judge thee, thou wicked servant. Thou knewest that I was an austere man, taking up that I laid not down, and reaping that I did not sow:

(23) Wherefore then gavest not thou my money into the bank, that at my coming I might have required mine own with usury?

(24) And he said unto them that stood by, Take from him the pound, and give it to him that hath ten pounds.

(25) (And they said unto him, Lord, he hath ten pounds.)

(26) For I say unto you, That unto every one which hath shall be given; and from him that hath not, even that he hath shall be taken away from him.

Laura said to read Luke 19 when planning a budget. This parable tells us to use wisely what we have. There should be no waste and no sloth in using what we have been given. We must carefully put it all to maximum use. Don't bury any of it. Put it all to work.

Laura was somewhat of an expert at budgeting. Maybe she had to be. In living on a little farm, a little had to go a long way. There was no room for waste. All income and increase had to be carefully used, and even the use of the land had to be budgeted: that is, its use had to be maximized.

With her expertise at budgeting, Laura became treasurer of the Farm Loan Board. She worked with farmers who were getting loans to work their farms, and she helped them with financial plans for their crops.

I helped a farmer figure out the value of his crops raised during the last season recently, and he was a very astonished person. Then when we added to that figure the amount he had received for livestock during the same period, he said: "It doesn't seem as if a man who had taken in that much off his farm would need a loan."

Laura Ingalls Wilder

Laura was a big advocate of getting a lot out of a little. Most of the Ozark farmers were small and struggling. Here is an example of a small farm which was carefully budgeted.

When Mr. Barton bought his 80-acre farm on the "post oak flats" near Mountain Grove, the people he met gave him the encouragement usually given to newcomers in the Ozarks. They told him the land was good for nothing, that he could not grow anything on it...

They soon found that there was more work on an 80-acre farm than they could handle, for while there were eight in the family, the six children were small, so it was decided to adjust the work to the family and 40 acres of the land, on which were the improvements, were sold for $2,500. Later 15 acres more were sold for $600. As the place had cost only $40 an acre, that left only $100 as the cost of the 25- acre farm that was kept.

These 25 acres of unimproved, poor land have been made into a truly remarkable little farm. During last season, it produced the following crops: 10 acres of corn, 400 bushels; 2 acres of oats, 20 bushels; 1 acre of millet hay, 2 tons; 1 acre of sorghum, 115 gallons of molasses; cowpeas, 100 bushels.

Besides these crops there was a 5-acre truck patch which furnished a good income thru the summer, but of which no account was kept. There has been sold off the place this last season livestock amounting to $130, poultry $15, butter $250 and grain $35. The rest of the grain was still on the place when this was written. Not bad for a 25-acre farm, is it?

Laura Ingalls Wilder

Laura and Manly tried to use the same type of budgeting and planning on their own little farm. They had to.

The primary lesson of the parable of the pounds is spiritual. It is similar to the parable of the talents in Matthew 25.

Mat 25:14-30 ESV
(14) "For it will be like a man going on a journey, who called his servants and entrusted to them his property.
(15) To one he gave five talents, to another two, to another one, to each according to his ability. Then he went away.
(16) He who had received the five talents went at once and traded with them, and he made five talents more.
(17) So also he who had the two talents made two talents more.
(18) But he who had received the one talent went and dug in the ground and hid his master's money.
(19) Now after a long time the master of those servants came and settled accounts with them.
(20) And he who had received the five talents came forward, bringing five talents more, saying, 'Master, you delivered to me five talents; here I have made five talents more.'
(21) His master said to him, 'Well done, good and faithful servant. You have been faithful over a little; I

will set you over much. Enter into the joy of your master.'

(22) And he also who had the two talents came forward, saying, 'Master, you delivered to me two talents; here I have made two talents more.'

(23) His master said to him, 'Well done, good and faithful servant. You have been faithful over a little; I will set you over much. Enter into the joy of your master.'

(24) He also who had received the one talent came forward, saying, 'Master, I knew you to be a hard man, reaping where you did not sow, and gathering where you scattered no seed,

(25) so I was afraid, and I went and hid your talent in the ground. Here you have what is yours.'

(26) But his master answered him, 'You wicked and slothful servant! You knew that I reap where I have not sown and gather where I scattered no seed?

(27) Then you ought to have invested my money with the bankers, and at my coming I should have received what was my own with interest.

(28) So take the talent from him and give it to him who has the ten talents.

(29) For to everyone who has will more be given, and he will have an abundance. But from the one who has not, even what he has will be taken away.

(30) And cast the worthless servant into the outer darkness. In that place there will be weeping and gnashing of teeth.'

The first thing we notice about these parables is that there are two categories of people whom Christ condemned.

- First, they who are His enemies.

- Second, they who are His servants and do nothing.

Those who receive a well done from the Master are His servants who actually do something to serve Him.

Peter tells us something which relates to these parables.

> 1Pe 4:10 ESV
> (10) As each has received a gift, use it to serve one another, as good stewards of God's varied grace:

In budgeting our lives, we must be careful not to be selfish. Even in an uplifting setting, such as a small farm, we must be careful not to spend all our time on building our own nest. God gives us gifts, and those gifts are to be used in the service of God and others, not just ourselves.

> Luk 12:13-21 ESV
> (13) Someone in the crowd said to him, "Teacher, tell my brother to divide the inheritance with me."
> (14) But he said to him, "Man, who made me a judge or arbitrator over you?"
> (15) And he said to them, "Take care, and be on your guard against all covetousness, for one's life does not consist in the abundance of his possessions."
> (16) And he told them a parable, saying, "The land of a rich man produced plentifully,
> (17) and he thought to himself, 'What shall I do, for I have nowhere to store my crops?'
> (18) And he said, 'I will do this: I will tear down my barns and build larger ones, and there I will store all my grain and my goods.
> (19) And I will say to my soul, Soul, you have ample goods laid up for many years; relax, eat, drink, be merry.'
> (20) But God said to him, 'Fool! This night your soul is required of you, and the things you have prepared, whose will they be?'

(21) So is the one who lays up treasure for himself and is not rich toward God."

Laura quoted those verses in one of her articles, and commented:

> *We are so overwhelmed with things these days that our lives are all more or less cluttered. I believe it is this, rather than a shortness of time, that gives us that feeling of hurry and almost of helplessness. Everyone is hurrying and usually just a little late. Notice the faces of the people who rush past on the streets or on our country roads! They nearly all have a strained, harassed look, and anyone you meet will tell you there is no time for anything anymore.*
>
> *Laura Ingalls Wilder*

In our lives, we have to create physical increase to make a living. A follower of Christ, though, does not live for that physical increase. We live for Christ. Even if we have a small farm and try to make it successful, that is not the purpose of our lives. Ultimately the purpose of our lives is to increase God's kingdom, not our own little kingdoms.

In 586 BC the Babylonians burned the first temple and carried the Jews away to Babylon. After the Jews returned from their 70 year captivity in Babylon, they stopped rebuilding the second temple.

Why?

They were too busy working on their own places.

> Hag 1:2-14 WEB
> (2) "This is what Yahweh of Armies says: These people say, 'The time hasn't yet come, the time for Yahweh's house to be built.' "

---

(3) Then the Word of Yahweh came by Haggai, the prophet, saying,

(4) "Is it a time for you yourselves to dwell in your paneled houses, while this house lies waste?

(5) Now therefore this is what Yahweh of Armies says: Consider your ways.

(6) You have sown much, and bring in little. You eat, but you don't have enough. You drink, but you aren't filled with drink. You clothe yourselves, but no one is warm, and he who earns wages earns wages to put them into a bag with holes in it."

(7) This is what Yahweh of Armies says: "Consider your ways.

(8) Go up to the mountain, bring wood, and build the house. I will take pleasure in it, and I will be glorified," says Yahweh.

(9) "You looked for much, and, behold, it came to little; and when you brought it home, I blew it away. Why?" says Yahweh of Armies, "Because of my house that lies waste, while each of you is busy with his own house.

(10) Therefore for your sake the heavens withhold the dew, and the earth withholds its fruit.

(11) I called for a drought on the land, on the mountains, on the grain, on the new wine, on the oil, on that which the ground brings forth, on men, on livestock, and on all the labor of the hands."

(12) Then Zerubbabel, the son of Shealtiel, and Joshua, the son of Jehozadak, the high priest, with all the remnant of the people, obeyed the voice of Yahweh, their God, and the words of Haggai, the prophet, as Yahweh, their God, had sent him; and the people feared Yahweh.

(13) Then Haggai, Yahweh's messenger, spoke Yahweh's message to the people, saying, "I am with you," says Yahweh.

(14) Yahweh stirred up the spirit of Zerubbabel, the son of Shealtiel, governor of Judah, and the spirit of Joshua, the son of Jehozadak, the high priest, and the spirit of all the remnant of the people; and they came and worked on the house of Yahweh of Armies, their God.

Most people make that same mistake. They focus on their paneled houses, while ignoring the building of God's temple. God's temple is a spiritual temple.

Eph 2:19-22 ESV
(19) So then you are no longer strangers and aliens, but you are fellow citizens with the saints and members of the household of God,
(20) built on the foundation of the apostles and prophets, Christ Jesus himself being the cornerstone,
(21) in whom the whole structure, being joined together, grows into a holy temple in the Lord.
(22) In him you also are being built together into a dwelling place for God by the Spirit.

Most people work most of their lives trying to get more for themselves. They do that as if they are doing God a service. Constantly filling your own barns is not serving God.

Christ is the Master. We are the servants. He gives us gifts to use to increase His kingdom. Very few people budget very much of their time to increase that kingdom. That is very poor budgeting.

We must remember the manna principle. Each day enough manna fell for that day. Those who hoarded only got wormy manna. We cannot increase spiritually unless we take the time to work at that. The life that works only for getting and not for giving will be filled with wormy manna.

Your time is your life. You will spend your time on what you love. If you love self most, you will spend your time and your life getting increase for yourself. If you love God most, you will spend your time getting increase for Him.

Luk 19:11-26 ESV

(11) As they heard these things, he proceeded to tell a parable, because he was near to Jerusalem, and because they supposed that the kingdom of God was to appear immediately.

(12) He said therefore, "A nobleman went into a far country to receive for himself a kingdom and then return.

(13) Calling ten of his servants, he gave them ten minas, and said to them, 'Engage in business until I come.'

(14) But his citizens hated him and sent a delegation after him, saying, 'We do not want this man to reign over us.'

(15) When he returned, having received the kingdom, he ordered these servants to whom he had given the money to be called to him, that he might know what they had gained by doing business.

(16) The first came before him, saying, 'Lord, your mina has made ten minas more.'

(17) And he said to him, 'Well done, good servant! Because you have been faithful in a very little, you shall have authority over ten cities.

(18) And the second came, saying, 'Lord, your mina has made five minas.'

(19) And he said to him, 'And you are to be over five cities.'

(20) Then another came, saying, 'Lord, here is your mina, which I kept laid away in a handkerchief;

(21) for I was afraid of you, because you are a severe man. You take what you did not deposit, and reap what you did not sow.'

(22) He said to him, 'I will condemn you with your own words, you wicked servant! You knew that I was a

severe man, taking what I did not deposit and reaping what I did not sow?

(23) Why then did you not put my money in the bank, and at my coming I might have collected it with interest?'

(24) And he said to those who stood by, 'Take the mina from him, and give it to the one who has the ten minas.'

(25) And they said to him, 'Lord, he has ten minas!'

(26) 'I tell you that to everyone who has, more will be given, but from the one who has not, even what he has will be taken away.

Chapter Five

To live successfully with others, read Romans chapter 12

To live successfully with others,
read Romans chapter 12

Romans 12

Rom 12:1-21 KJ

(1) I beseech you therefore, brethren, by the mercies of God, that ye present your bodies a living sacrifice, holy, acceptable unto God, which is your reasonable service.

(2) And be not conformed to this world: but be ye transformed by the renewing of your mind, that ye may prove what is that good, and acceptable, and perfect, will of God.

(3) For I say, through the grace given unto me, to every man that is among you, not to think of himself more highly than he ought to think; but to think soberly, according as God hath dealt to every man the measure of faith.

(4) For as we have many members in one body, and all members have not the same office:

(5) So we, being many, are one body in Christ, and every one members one of another.

(6) Having then gifts differing according to the grace that is given to us, whether prophecy, let us prophesy according to the proportion of faith;

(7) Or ministry, let us wait on our ministering: or he that teacheth, on teaching;

(8) Or he that exhorteth, on exhortation: he that giveth, let him do it with simplicity; he that ruleth, with diligence; he that sheweth mercy, with cheerfulness.

(9) Let love be without dissimulation. Abhor that which is evil; cleave to that which is good.

(10) Be kindly affectioned one to another with brotherly love; in honour preferring one another;

(11) Not slothful in business; fervent in spirit; serving the Lord;

(12) Rejoicing in hope; patient in tribulation; continuing instant in prayer;

(13) Distributing to the necessity of saints; given to hospitality.

(14) Bless them which persecute you: bless, and curse not.

(15) Rejoice with them that do rejoice, and weep with them that weep.

(16) Be of the same mind one toward another. Mind not high things, but condescend to men of low estate. Be not wise in your own conceits.

(17) Recompense to no man evil for evil. Provide things honest in the sight of all men.

(18) If it be possible, as much as lieth in you, live peaceably with all men.

(19) Dearly beloved, avenge not yourselves, but rather give place unto wrath: for it is written, Vengeance is mine; I will repay, saith the Lord.

(20) Therefore if thine enemy hunger, feed him; if he thirst, give him drink: for in so doing thou shalt heap coals of fire on his head.

(21) Be not overcome of evil, but overcome evil with good.

Laura often wrote about getting along with people. It was said that she herself was tactful.

Tact does for life just what lubricating oil does for machinery. It makes the wheels run smoothly, and without it there is a great deal of friction and the possibility of a breakdown. Many a car on the way of life fails to make the trip as expected for lack of this lubricant.

Tact is a quality that may be acquired. It is only the other way of seeing and presenting a subject. There are always two sides to a thing, you know; and if one side is disagreeable, the reverse is quite apt to be very pleasant. The tactful person may see both sides but uses the pleasant one.

Laura Ingalls Wilder

Peggy Dennis, who knew Laura in Mansfield, said this about Laura's dealings with people.

One time Almanzo was feeling poorly. Neta Seal asked him if there was anything she could do for him. Almanzo said he would like to have a double crust pineapple pie, so Neta said she would fix him one. She did and took it to him. Then, in turn, Laura brought Neta some glazed fruits. It was like she didn't want you to do something for them unless she could do something in return for you.

From *Laura Ingalls' Friends Remember Her.*

Laura herself talked about that custom, of always repaying a favor.

When a neighbor does us a favor, we show our appreciation of it by doing him a favor in return. Then when the Lord showers favors upon us, how much more should we try to show our gratitude in such ways acceptable to Him, remembering always the words of Christ, "Inasmuch as ye have done it unto one of the least of these my brethren, ye have done it unto me."

Laura Ingalls Wilder

And she talked about how to avoid tangled misunderstandings.

A person who cannot be depended upon by others, in time becomes unable to depend upon himself. It seems in some subtle way to undermine and weaken the character when we do not hold ourselves strictly responsible for what we say.

And what a tangle it makes of all our undertakings when people do not keep their promises. How much pleasanter it would be, and how much more would be accomplished, if we did not give our word unless we intended to keep it, so that we would all know what we could depend on.

Laura Ingalls Wilder

Laura got along well with people. One of the reasons she did was that she read Romans 12. This is one of the great sections of the Bible in discussing humility and service.

First, humility:

- not to think of himself more highly than he ought to think;
- in honor preferring one another;
- don't be wise in your own conceits;

Consider this. The famous Little House author, praised as a great writer, who from a small town in the Ozarks had gained nationwide notoriety, fed her mind with these thoughts: to not think more highly of herself than she ought, to prefer others over herself, and not to be wise in her own conceits.

Important people often become pompous. Herod did.

> Act 12:20-23 ESV
> (20) Now Herod was angry with the people of Tyre and Sidon, and they came to him with one accord, and

having persuaded Blastus, the king's chamberlain, they asked for peace, because their country depended on the king's country for food.

(21) On an appointed day Herod put on his royal robes, took his seat upon the throne, and delivered an oration to them.

(22) And the people were shouting, "The voice of a god, and not of a man!"

(23) Immediately an angel of the Lord struck him down, because he did not give God the glory, and he was eaten by worms and breathed his last.

One of the most difficult challenges anyone can face is to be an important person and not think that you are. George Washington was one of the most amazing men in all history. He walked away from being king of the new United States – twice: right after the revolution, and after his presidency.

Important people often become pompous. Laura didn't.

It was said of Laura that she really didn't like to receive visitors who only came to see the famous author. The reason was that they weren't really coming to visit her as a person -- only to see a famous person.

Think about this little old lady, called Half Pint by her pa because she was never very large, famous for her God given talent to tell stories of her life and family, reading Romans 12. Can we see her sitting in her rocker, sometimes not answering when the souvenir seekers banged on her door, her feet barely hitting the floor, her hair all white from age, known nationwide, yet reading carefully to herself – "don't be wise in your own conceits?" Not reading articles about how great her stories were or how they have changed the lives of multiple thousands for the better, but reading to "prefer others in honor."

That's quite a sight.

Paul said to give ourselves to service. Laura did give a spiritual service when she wrote her Little House books. In a world today that badly needs edifying, her books are still doing that. In a society that is pulled down in ways not imagined when she was alive, her books still lift us up. In a world that is filling up with evil, her books give us a measure of good, good being love for God and others.

May more of us be able to give such a spiritual service to God, to present ourselves a living sacrifice, not dedicated to ourselves, but seeking to do the perfect will of God.

This writing by Paul in Romans 12 focuses on two areas:

- one, not seeking to attack others when they attack you;
- and two, not seeking to exalt oneself over others.

This is the way Christ was. That is the way Paul was.

Who was Paul?

Paul was a servant of Christ, who spread the gospel of peace. For that, he suffered this:

2Co 11:24-28 ESV
- Five times I received at the hands of the Jews forty lashes less one.
- Three times I was beaten with rods.
- Once I was stoned.
- Three times I was shipwrecked;
- a night and a day I was adrift at sea;
- on frequent journeys, in danger from rivers, danger from robbers, danger from my own people, danger from Gentiles, danger in the city, danger in the wilderness, danger at sea, danger from false brothers;
- in toil and hardship, through many a sleepless night,

- in hunger and thirst, often without food, in cold and exposure.
- And, apart from other things, there is the daily pressure on me of my anxiety for all the churches.

After all that, Paul said:

- Rejoice in hope, be patient in tribulation, be constant in prayer.
- Bless those who persecute you; bless and do not curse them.
- Live in harmony with one another. Do not be haughty, but associate with the lowly. Never be wise in your own sight.
- Repay no one evil for evil, but give thought to do what is honorable in the sight of all.
- Live peaceably with all.
- Beloved, never avenge yourselves, but leave it to the wrath of God, for it is written, "Vengeance is mine, I will repay, says the Lord."
- To the contrary, "if your enemy is hungry, feed him; if he is thirsty, give him something to drink; for by so doing you will heap burning coals on his head."
- Do not be overcome by evil, but overcome evil with good.

The Bible is such a marvelous work. How foolish people are today when they cast it off as myth. They presume to know its source and meaning without ever knowing it!

Look at this marvelous section of Romans. Paul suffered constant persecution and was finally martyred for preaching peace and the Prince of Peace. In today's America people are constantly clamoring for their rights. We live in the most litigious society ever. Nearly everybody is ready to attack when they think someone has done them wrong. They demand their rights!

But Paul, beaten, stoned and wrecked said –

I demand my rights! Somebody's gonna pay for this!

No – he said: repay no one evil for evil, bless your persecutors, and feed your enemy.

While the Messiah was being killed, He was praying for those who were killing Him. When Stephen was stoned, he asked God not to hold those rocks against the throwers.

This is the mind of God. This is the way of life. Writings in the Bible like Romans 12 are the epitome of human literature. This is as good as it gets. These thoughts do not come merely from the pens of men, but from God Himself.

> Rom 12:1-21 ESV
> I appeal to you therefore, brothers, by the mercies of God, to present your bodies as a living sacrifice, holy and acceptable to God, which is your spiritual worship.
>
> Do not be conformed to this world, but be transformed by the renewal of your mind, that by testing you may discern what is the will of God, what is good and acceptable and perfect.
>
> For by the grace given to me I say to everyone among you not to think of himself more highly than he ought to think, but to think with sober judgment, each according to the measure of faith that God has assigned.
>
> For as in one body we have many members, and the members do not all have the same function, so we, though many, are one body in Christ, and individually members one of another.
>
> Having gifts that differ according to the grace given to us, let us use them:

- if prophecy, in proportion to our faith;
- if service, in our serving;
- the one who teaches, in his teaching;
- the one who exhorts, in his exhortation;
- the one who contributes, in generosity;
- the one who leads, with zeal;
- the one who does acts of mercy, with cheerfulness.

Let love be genuine.
Abhor what is evil;
hold fast to what is good.

Love one another with brotherly affection.
Outdo one another in showing honor.

Do not be slothful in zeal, be fervent in spirit, serve the Lord.

Rejoice in hope,
be patient in tribulation,
be constant in prayer.

Contribute to the needs of the saints and seek to show hospitality.
Bless those who persecute you; bless and do not curse them.
Rejoice with those who rejoice, weep with those who weep.
Live in harmony with one another.
Do not be haughty, but associate with the lowly.
Never be wise in your own sight.

Repay no one evil for evil, but give thought to do what is honorable in the sight of all.
If possible, so far as it depends on you, live peaceably with all.

Beloved, never avenge yourselves, but leave it to the wrath of God, for it is written, "Vengeance is mine, I will repay, says the Lord."

To the contrary, "if your enemy is hungry, feed him; if he is thirsty, give him something to drink; for by so doing you will heap burning coals on his head."

Do not be overcome by evil, but overcome evil with good.

Chapter Six

Sick or in pain, read 91 Psalm

Sick or in pain read 91 Psalm

Psalm 91

Psa 91:1-16, KJ

(1) He that dwelleth in the secret place of the most High shall abide under the shadow of the Almighty.

(2) I will say of the LORD, He is my refuge and my fortress: my God; in him will I trust.

(3) Surely he shall deliver thee from the snare of the fowler, and from the noisome pestilence.

(4) He shall cover thee with his feathers, and under his wings shalt thou trust: his truth shall be thy shield and buckler.

(5) Thou shalt not be afraid for the terror by night; nor for the arrow that flieth by day;

(6) Nor for the pestilence that walketh in darkness; nor for the destruction that wasteth at noonday.

(7) A thousand shall fall at thy side, and ten thousand at thy right hand; but it shall not come nigh thee.

(8) Only with thine eyes shalt thou behold and see the reward of the wicked.

(9) Because thou hast made the LORD, which is my refuge, even the most High, thy habitation;

(10) There shall no evil befall thee, neither shall any plague come nigh thy dwelling.

(11) For he shall give his angels charge over thee, to keep thee in all thy ways.

(12) They shall bear thee up in their hands, lest thou dash thy foot against a stone.

(13) Thou shalt tread upon the lion and adder: the young lion and the dragon shalt thou trample under feet.

(14) Because he hath set his love upon me, therefore will I deliver him: I will set him on high, because he hath known my name.

(15) He shall call upon me, and I will answer him: I will be with him in trouble; I will deliver him, and honour him.

(16) With long life will I satisfy him, and shew him my salvation.

Laura said to read Psalm 91 when sick or in pain.

> *Sometimes we recognize as a special blessing what heretofore we have taken without a thought as a matter of course, as when we recover from a serious illness: just a breath drawn free from pain is a matter of rejoicing. If we have been crippled and then are whole again, the blessed privilege of walking forth free and unhindered seems a gift from the "gods." We must have been hungry to properly appreciate food, and we never love our friends as we should until they have been taken from us.*

> *Laura Ingalls Wilder*

In late winter in 1888, when they lived on their homestead near De Smet, Laura thought she had caught a bad cold. She went to bed and little Rose went to stay with Ma Ingalls.

Laura did not get better, but worse. A doctor was called out, and he said that she did not have a cold at all. She had diphtheria.

Diphtheria is a serious illness. It is passed by direct contact with the bacteria from others who have the disease, and has a usual incubation period of two to five days. Somehow Laura had picked up the bacteria and caught that dreaded disease.

Manly cared for Laura, and with Rose staying at the Ingalls, she did not get sick. But Manly did.

So both Laura and Manly were bedfast with dangerous diphtheria at the same time.

They were then cared for by Manly's brother Royal. He was not married and was willing to put his own health at risk by caring for them. Laura described his care as crude and her and Manly's sick days as being miserable and feverish.

Her case was bad. Manly's was relatively light. Slowly they began to recover.

Soon Manly thought he was well enough to begin working again. Of course, they had already had difficulty keeping up with their workload, and when they got sick, they got behind. Manly went back to work as quickly as he could.

One of the effects of diphtheria is to damage the nervous system. One morning Manly's legs were numb and partially paralyzed. The doctor said he had suffered a stroke –

from working too hard too soon after his illness.

Right after that, Manly could walk, but if he stubbed his toe on the smallest obstacle he fell down. If there was any little something in his way, he could not step over it but had to shuffle around it.

His hands didn't work well, either. He could not buckle the leather harness on his beloved horses. Laura had to do that for him. He could drive by clutching the reins in his clumsy hands.

With all his determined effort to strengthen himself, Manly gradually improved. For the rest of his life, though, he walked with a limp, and often a cane.

In 1888, when the winter was over, the diphtheria had laid Laura and Manly up and put them behind on their work. They had a doctor bill that they had to pay. Harvest, if it came, would be way off in the fall. They had nothing to live on until then. And Manly, the farmer boy who loved to farm, was partially paralyzed.

Notice these loving phrases from Psalm 91 which Laura would have read when they were sick and in pain:

- "Rest in the shadow of the Almighty;"
- "Cover you with His feathers,"
- "Under His wings you will take refuge."
- "He will put His angels in charge of you to guard you in all your ways."

Laura's love for beautiful writing would also have led her to this psalm.

The *Adam Clarke Commentary* says of Psalm 91:

> "It is allowed to be one of the finest Psalms in the whole collection. Of it Simon de Muis has said: 'It is one of the most excellent works of this kind which has ever appeared. It is impossible to imagine any thing more solid, more beautiful, more profound, or more ornamented. Could the Latin or any modern languages express thoroughly all the beauties and elegancies as well of the words as of the sentences, it would not be difficult to persuade the reader that we have no poem, either in Greek or Latin, comparable to this Hebrew ode.'"

The Bible does not say who wrote Psalm 91. The Targum, a Jewish paraphrase, says that David wrote it. The Septuagint, Vulgate Latin, Syriac, Arabic, and Ethiopic versions agree with that. Further, it is thought that David wrote this psalm after his sin of numbering Israel, which caused a pestilence to come upon the nation.

Let's look closely at this psalm.

> Ps 91 WEB
> (1) He who dwells in the secret place of the Most High will rest in the shadow of the Almighty.
>
> (2) I will say of Yahweh,
>   He is my refuge and my fortress;
>   My God, in whom I trust.

Whoever you trust is your God.

It is said that David wrote this psalm after he had numbered Israel. Numbering Israel was a great sin by David, which is often hard for people to understand.

That account is in II Samuel 24.

> 2Sa24 WEB
> (1) Again the anger of Yahweh was kindled against Israel, and he moved David against them, saying, Go, number Israel and Judah.

Notice that Yahweh was already angry with Israel. Why would God get mad at Israel, His chosen people from His servant Abraham?

Always that was because they were forsaking Him. When He punished them, He wasn't just picking on them. He was purifying them.

The anger of Yahweh was against Israel, so he let David do what came naturally with human nature. David exalted himself.

> 2Sa24
>
> (2) The king said to Joab the captain of the army, who was with him, Go now back and forth through all the tribes of Israel, from Dan even to Beersheba, and number you the people, that I may know the sum of the people.
>
> (3) Joab said to the king, Now Yahweh your God add to the people, however many they may be, one hundred times; and may the eyes of my lord the king see it: but why does my lord the king delight in this thing?

Joab was not always a man of great wisdom. He killed Abner, a great man in the service of Saul, and he killed Absalom, David's son, in direct defiance of the king's order. But in this case, Joab showed great wisdom. Joab realized David's great sin in numbering Israel and tried to dissuade the king.

> 2Sa24
>
> (4) Notwithstanding, the king's word prevailed against Joab, and against the captains of the army. Joab and the captains of the army went out from the presence of the king, to number the people of Israel.
>
> (5) They passed over the Jordan, and encamped in Aroer, on the right side of the city that is in the middle of the valley of Gad, and to Jazer:
>
> (6) then they came to Gilead, and to the land of Tahtim Hodshi; and they came to Dan Jaan, and around to Sidon,
>
> (7) and came to the stronghold of Tyre, and to all the cities of the Hivites, and of the Canaanites; and they went out to the south of Judah, at Beersheba.
>
> (8) So when they had gone back and forth through all the land, they came to Jerusalem at the end of nine months and twenty days.

(9) Joab gave up the sum of the numbering of the people to the king: and there were in Israel eight hundred thousand valiant men who drew the sword; and the men of Judah were five hundred thousand men.

There it was. The ten tribes of Israel had 800,000 good soldiers and Judah had 500,000. All together King David had an incredible army of 1,300,000 valiant men.

Then, just as David learned of his great power, he saw his great sin.

2Sa 24
(10) David's heart struck him after that he had numbered the people.

You will recall that when David committed adultery with Bathsheba, the prophet Nathan had to point out David's sin. Here David is able to recognize his own sin. In both cases, his repentance was immediate and deep.

2Sa 24
(10) David's heart struck him after that he had numbered the people. David said to Yahweh, I have sinned greatly in that which I have done: but now, Yahweh, put away, I beg you, the iniquity of your servant; for I have done very foolishly.
(11) When David rose up in the morning, the word of Yahweh came to the prophet Gad, David's seer, saying,
(12) Go and speak to David, Thus says Yahweh, I offer you three things: choose one of them, that I may do it to you.
(13) So Gad came to David, and told him, and said to him, Shall seven years of famine come to you in your land? or will you flee three months before your foes while they pursue you? or shall there be three days' pestilence in your land? Now answer, and consider what answer I shall return to him who sent me.

David said that he had sinned greatly. What was that great sin? Is taking a census sin? Few can understand the depth of the problem here. Obviously there was a big problem with God, for Israel suffered a great pestilence because of this sin.

> 2Sa 24
>
> (14) David said to Gad, I am in distress. Let us fall now into the hand of Yahweh; for his mercies are great; and let me not fall into the hand of man.
>
> (15) So Yahweh sent a pestilence on Israel from the morning even to the time appointed; and there died of the people from Dan even to Beersheba seventy thousand men.

God considered this sin so great that 70,000 died from the plague. David had exalted himself by the number of his people, and he was humbled at how quickly they could be lost.

That great sin which caused such a penalty was looking to serve self instead of looking to serve God. Since Yahweh was angry with Israel to begin with, surely the sin was not just David's, but spread throughout Israel. King David, he who had killed Goliath with Yahweh and a stone, he who had displaced King Saul by never lifting a hand against him – King David sought to serve himself by his big, big army.

When David numbered Israel, he did not do it to glorify God. He did it to glorify himself. Such self serving is the pit and epitome of Satan's spirit. David had it, Israel had it, and they both got it – trouble.

However, once David realized his sin, then he realized his sin. When given the choice of seven years of famine, or being chased by his enemies, or suffering a pestilence at the hands of God –

David chose God. Even when he was being punished by God, he looked to God for deliverance.

He learned the lesson. And he was right.

> 2Sa 24
> (16) When the angel stretched out his hand toward Jerusalem to destroy it, Yahweh relented of the disaster, and said to the angel who destroyed the people, It is enough; now stay your hand.

Yahweh did have mercy, and called off the pestilence.

Psalm 91 continues:

> Psa 91 WEB
> (3) For he will deliver you from the snare of the fowler, and from the deadly pestilence.
> (4) He will cover you with his feathers. Under his wings you will take refuge. His faithfulness is your shield and rampart.
> (5) You shall not be afraid of the terror by night, nor of the arrow that flies by day;
> (6) nor of the pestilence that walks in darkness, nor of the destruction that wastes at noonday.
> (7) A thousand may fall at your side, and ten thousand at your right hand; but it will not come near you.
> (8) You will only look with your eyes, and see the recompense of the wicked.

Undoubtedly what happened to those 70,000 who died in the pestilence was the recompense of the wicked. God knows what he is doing in every detail.

Speaking of the wicked, Satan quoted part of Psalm 91, the great psalm of God's refuge, to Christ. The underlined portion below was referred to by Satan.

> Psa 91 ESV
> (9) Because you have made Yahweh your refuge, and the Most High your dwelling place,

(10) no evil shall happen to you, neither shall any plague come near your dwelling.
(11) For he will put his angels in charge of you, to guard you in all your ways.
(12) They will bear you up in their hands, so that you won't dash your foot against a stone.

That was part of the great temptation, when Satan tried to get Christ to sin. Notice how the Adversary, which is what Satan means, attacked Christ.

> Mat 4 Modern King James
> (1) Then Jesus was led by the Spirit up into the wilderness, to be tempted by the Devil.
> (2) And when He had fasted forty days and forty nights, He was afterwards hungry.
> (3) And when the tempter came to Him, he said, If You are the Son of God, command that these stones be made bread.
> (4) But He answered and said, It is written, "Man shall not live by bread alone, but by every word that proceeds out of the mouth of God."
> (5) Then the Devil took Him up into the holy city and set Him upon a pinnacle of the Temple.
> (6) And he said to Him, If you are the Son of God, cast yourself down. For it is written, "He shall give His angels charge concerning You, and in their hands they shall bear You up, lest at any time You dash Your foot against a stone."
> (7) Jesus said to him, It is written again, "You shall not tempt the Lord your God."
> (8) Again, the Devil took Him up into a very high mountain and showed Him all the kingdoms of the world and their glory.
> (9) And he said to Him, All these things I will give You if You will fall down and worship me.

(10) Then Jesus said to him, Go, Satan! For it is written, "You shall worship the Lord your God, and Him only you shall serve."

When he quoted from Psalm 91, Satan dared Christ to jump from a pinnacle of the temple, because it was promised that the angels would bear Him up.

Notice the pattern.

David had exalted himself in counting his soldiers, just to show how great he was, or how great God had made him. Perhaps after that he wrote Psalm 91.

If Christ had thrown himself off the temple, just to show that the angels would catch him, he would have made the same mistake as David. He would just have been showing off how great he was, and how great God had made him. Jumping off the temple would not have served to glorify God, but to glorify self.

No wonder Satan quoted from Psalm 91, one of the greatest psalms about making God your trust. He was daring Christ not to do that.

It can seem like such a small thing. David counted Israel's army, and 70,000 died in a pestilence. And if Christ had accepted Satan's dare and just jumped off the temple to show He could do it – all of mankind would have been lost by that sin.

Christ is our salvation. If we can receive that, we will call, and He will answer. We don't have to count our army, and we don't have to jump off anything just to prove it.

A disbeliever cannot understand what is in this psalm. He cannot feel the serenity of being under the wings of the Creator of everything, and he cannot feel the living love of God in a work of beauty such as this.

Laura could. In spite of their illness, both she and Manly lived past ninety, helped in part by Psalm 91.

> Psa 91:1-16 WEB
> (1) He who dwells in the secret place of the Most High will rest in the shadow of the Almighty.
> (2) I will say of Yahweh, "He is my refuge and my fortress; my God, in whom I trust."
> (3) For he will deliver you from the snare of the fowler, and from the deadly pestilence.
> (4) He will cover you with his feathers. Under his wings you will take refuge. His faithfulness is your shield and rampart.
> (5) You shall not be afraid of the terror by night, nor of the arrow that flies by day;
> (6) nor of the pestilence that walks in darkness, nor of the destruction that wastes at noonday.
> (7) A thousand may fall at your side, and ten thousand at your right hand; but it will not come near you.
> (8) You will only look with your eyes, and see the recompense of the wicked.
> (9) Because you have made Yahweh your refuge, and the Most High your dwelling place,
> (10) no evil shall happen to you, neither shall any plague come near your dwelling.
> (11) For he will put his angels in charge of you, to guard you in all your ways.
> (12) They will bear you up in their hands, so that you won't dash your foot against a stone.
> (13) You will tread on the lion and cobra. You will trample the young lion and the serpent underfoot.
> (14) "Because he has set his love on me, therefore I will deliver him. I will set him on high, because he has known my name.

(15) He will call on me, and I will answer him. I will be with him in trouble. I will deliver him, and honor him. (16) I will satisfy him with long life, and show him my salvation."

Chapter Seven

When you travel carry with you

121 Psalm

When you travel carry with you 121 Psalm

Psalm 121

Psa 121:1-8 KJ

(1) I will lift up mine eyes unto the hills, from whence cometh my help.

(2) My help cometh from the LORD, which made heaven and earth.

(3) He will not suffer thy foot to be moved: he that keepeth thee will not slumber.

(4) Behold, he that keepeth Israel shall neither slumber nor sleep.

(5) The LORD is thy keeper: the LORD is thy shade upon thy right hand.

(6) The sun shall not smite thee by day, nor the moon by night.

(7) The LORD shall preserve thee from all evil: he shall preserve thy soul.

(8) The LORD shall preserve thy going out and thy coming in from this time forth, and even for evermore.

Laura said to read Psalm 121 when traveling. The last verse of the psalm says that God will preserve your going out and coming in – which is traveling.

When Laura said that she read this verse while she was traveling, that shows that she took her Bible with her on trips. She could not have read Psalm 121 when she was traveling unless she had a Bible to read. That shows a deep love and respect for the Word of God.

A big trip that Laura took – perhaps her biggest -- was to the world's fair in San Francisco in 1915. Her daughter Rose lived in San Francisco then and talked Laura into visiting her while the world's fair was in progress.

In 1915 the cavalry was just beginning to be outmoded by motorized tanks in the Great War in Europe. On the streets of the US, motor cars were just beginning to putter around. Most people still traveled locally by horse power – that's two words, not one. When people traveled long distance they went by train.

In 1869, two years after Laura's birth, the first railroad track all the way across the continent had been finished. In 1915, when Laura was 48, she took the train over much of that continent, from Mansfield, Missouri to San Francisco – all by herself. Manly had to take care of the farm, with its crops and animals, while half pint Laura, as her Pa had called her, took the train halfway across America. From Mansfield to San Francisco is about 2,000 miles, a big trip for a little lady in 1915.

To start her trip, Laura almost missed the train from Mansfield. Later she had an unexpected overnight layover in Denver. She met a number of strange gentlemen on the way, some stranger than others. It was far more common for men to travel by themselves than women. And Laura said en route that if she had known the trip would be so hard, she would not have gone.

So we can assume with some confidence that in 1915, on her train trip halfway across the United States, all by herself, Laura would have felt some apprehension. We can also assume that on that nervous trip, Laura read Psalm 121.

The *Sound of Music* is perhaps the most popular musical motion picture of all time. Near the end of that movie, the Von Trapp family is being pursued by the Nazis and is hiding in a Catholic abbey. They are unsure how to get away, when one of the nuns cites the first verse of Psalm 121 –

"I will lift up mine eyes unto the hills, from whence cometh my help."

The Von Trapps look up, and escape on foot through the mountains to Switzerland.

In the World English Bible, the first part of the psalm reads,

> (1) I will lift up my eyes to the hills.
> Where does my help come from?
> (2) My help comes from Yahweh,
> who made heaven and earth.

Jerusalem is in the hills. The Bible often uses the phrase to "go up to Jerusalem." Jerusalem has an elevation of 2550 feet, and Psalm 48 says:

> Psa 48:1-3 WEB
> (1) Great is Yahweh, and greatly to be praised, in the city of our God, in his holy mountain
> (2) Beautiful in elevation, the joy of the whole earth, is Mount Zion, on the north sides, the city of the great King.

> Also Psalm 125:2 WEB says,
> (2) As the mountains surround Jerusalem, so Yahweh surrounds his people from this time forth and forevermore.

Abraham once took a trip, and at the end of that trip he looked up and saw Mount Moriah, the hills which would become Jerusalem, from whence would come Abraham's help.

> Gen 22:1-13 WEB
> (1) It happened after these things, that God tested Abraham, and said to him, "Abraham!" He said, "Here I am."

(2) He said, "Now take your son, your only son, whom you love, even Isaac, and go into the land of Moriah. Offer him there for a burnt offering on one of the mountains which I will tell you of."

(3) Abraham rose early in the morning, and saddled his donkey, and took two of his young men with him, and Isaac his son. He split the wood for the burnt offering, and rose up, and went to the place of which God had told him.

(4) <u>On the third day Abraham lifted up his eyes, and saw the place far off.</u>

(5) Abraham said to his young men, "Stay here with the donkey. The boy and I will go yonder. We will worship, and come back to you."

(6) Abraham took the wood of the burnt offering and laid it on Isaac his son. He took in his hand the fire and the knife. They both went together.

(7) Isaac spoke to Abraham his father, and said, "My father?" He said, "Here I am, my son." He said, "Here is the fire and the wood, but where is the lamb for a burnt offering?"

(8) Abraham said, "God will provide himself the lamb for a burnt offering, my son." So they both went together.

(9) They came to the place which God had told him of. Abraham built the altar there, and laid the wood in order, bound Isaac his son, and laid him on the altar, on the wood.

(10) Abraham stretched forth his hand, and took the knife to kill his son.

(11) The angel of Yahweh called to him out of the sky, and said, "Abraham, Abraham!" He said, "Here I am."

(12) He said, "Don't lay your hand on the boy, neither do anything to him. For now I know that you fear God, seeing you have not withheld your son, your only son, from me."

(13) Abraham lifted up his eyes, and looked, and saw that behind him was a ram caught in the thicket by his horns. Abraham went and took the ram, and offered him up for a burnt offering instead of his son.

When Abraham was on that fateful trip, to sacrifice his only son by his true wife, on the third day he looked up to the hills, from whence came his help.

Psalm 121 is one of the fifteen psalms of degrees, from Psalm 120 through 134. They are considered Pilgrim Psalms, to be sung on the journey to Jerusalem to keep the three festival seasons of Passover, Pentecost and Tabernacles. The festivals were the times of the year when God's people were closest to Him. They left their normal work and spent that time worshiping God.

Joseph and Mary did that.

> Luk 2:41-49 ESV
> (41) Now his parents went to Jerusalem every year at the Feast of the Passover.
> (42) And when he was twelve years old, they went up according to custom.
> (43) And when the feast was ended, as they were returning, the boy Jesus stayed behind in Jerusalem. His parents did not know it,
> (44) but supposing him to be in the group they went a day's journey, but then they began to search for him among their relatives and acquaintances,
> (45) and when they did not find him, they returned to Jerusalem, searching for him.
>
> (46) After three days they found him in the temple, sitting among the teachers, listening to them and asking them questions.
> (47) And all who heard him were amazed at his understanding and his answers.

(48) And when his parents saw him, they were astonished. And his mother said to him, "Son, why have you treated us so? Behold, your father and I have been searching for you in great distress."
(49) And he said to them, "Why were you looking for me? Did you not know that I must be in my Father's house?"

As they traveled up to Jerusalem for Passover that year, Christ and his family may well have sung Psalm 121.

Later, when Christ came to Jerusalem for the last time in his earthly form –

He who was pictured by Isaac being on the altar,

going up for the feast of Passover and His own sacrifice,

may have sung this psalm,

as He lifted His eyes,

to where His help would come from.

Psa 121:1-8 WEB
(1) I will lift up my eyes to the hills.
Where does my help come from?
(2) My help comes from Yahweh,
who made heaven and earth.
(3) He will not allow your foot to be moved.
He who keeps you will not slumber.
(4) Behold, he who keeps Israel
will neither slumber nor sleep.
(5) Yahweh is your keeper.
Yahweh is your shade on your right hand.
(6) The sun will not harm you by day,
nor the moon by night.

(7) Yahweh will keep you from all evil.
He will keep your soul.
(8) Yahweh will keep your going out and your coming in, from this time forth, and forevermore.

Chapter Eight

When very weary read

Matthew 11:28 & 30

and

Romans 8:31 to 39

Matthew 11:28 & 30

Mat 11:28 & 30 KJ
(28) Come unto me, all ye that labour and are heavy laden, and I will give you rest.
(30) For my yoke is easy, and my burden is light.

Romans 8:31 – 39

Rom 8:31-39 KJ
(31) What shall we then say to these things? If God be for us, who can be against us?
(32) He that spared not his own Son, but delivered him up for us all, how shall he not with him also freely give us all things?
(33) Who shall lay any thing to the charge of God's elect? It is God that justifieth.
(34) Who is he that condemneth? It is Christ that died, yea rather, that is risen again, who is even at the right hand of God, who also maketh intercession for us.
(35) Who shall separate us from the love of Christ? shall tribulation, or distress, or persecution, or famine, or nakedness, or peril, or sword?
(36) As it is written, For thy sake we are killed all the day long; we are accounted as sheep for the slaughter.
(37) Nay, in all these things we are more than conquerors through him that loved us.

(38) For I am persuaded, that neither death, nor life, nor angels, nor principalities, nor powers, nor things present, nor things to come,

(39) Nor height, nor depth, nor any other creature, shall be able to separate us from the love of God, which is in Christ Jesus our Lord.

We all get weary, and as we get older, we get wearier more often. There is a physical weariness and a spiritual weariness. If you are spiritually weary, then you will also be physically weary.

When Laura and Manly came to the Ozarks and Rocky Ridge Farm, life did not suddenly turn easy for them. Besides working at Rocky Ridge, they cut wood, sold kerosene, took a house in town and boarded workers to try to earn enough money to stay alive. Such a constant scrabble, not just from month to month but from year to year, can tend to make a person weary.

The spring rush is almost upon us. The little chickens, the garden, the spring sewing and house-cleaning will be on our hands soon, and the worst of it is, they will all come together unless we have been very wise in our planning.

It almost makes one feel like the farmer's wife who called up the stairs to awaken the hired girl on a Monday morning. "Liza Jane," she called, "come hurry and get up and get the breakfast. This is wash day, and here it is almost 6 o'clock and the washing not done yet. Tomorrow is ironing day and the ironing not touched; next day is churning day and it's not begun, and here the week is half gone and nothing done yet."

Laura Ingalls Wilder

There used to be a saying: How are you going to keep them down on the farm?

In the last century, Americans left the farms in droves. They did that because the life was so hard, constantly working as long as the sun shone, at hard, physical, exhausting work.

Here are Laura and Manly reflecting on how hard their parents worked.

> *The Man of the Place and I were sitting cozily by the fire. The evening lamp was lighted and the day's papers and the late magazines were scattered over the table. But though we each held in our hands our favorite publications, we were not reading. We were grumbling about the work we had to do and saying all the things usually said at such times.*
>
> *"People used to have time to live and enjoy themselves, but there is no time anymore for anything but work, work, work."*
>
> *Oh, we threshed it all over as everyone does when they get that kind of grouch, and then we sat in silence. I was wishing I had lived altogether in those good old days when people had time for things they wanted to do.*
>
> *What the Man of the Place was thinking, I do not know; but I was quite surprised at the point at which he had arrived, when he remarked out of the silence, in a rather meek voice, "I never realized how much work my father did. Why, one winter he sorted five hundred bushels of potatoes after supper by lantern light. He sold them for $1.50 a bushel in the spring, too, but he must have got blamed tired of sorting potatoes down cellar every night until he had handled more than five hundred bushels of them."*

"What did your mother do while your father was sorting potatoes?" I asked.

"Oh, she sewed and knit," said the Man of the Place. "She made all our clothes, coats and pants, undergarments for father and us boys as well as everything she and the girls wore, and she knit all our socks and mittens – shag mittens for the men folks, do you remember, all fuzzy on the outside? She didn't have time enough in the day to do all the work and so she sewed and knit at night."

I looked down at the magazine in my hand and remembered how my mother was always sewing or knitting by the evening lamp. I realized that I had never done so except now and then in cases of emergency.

But the Man of the Place was still talking. "Mother did all her own sewing by hand then," he said, "and she spun her own yarn and wove her own cloth. Father harvested his grain by hand with a sickle and cut his hay with a scythe. I do wonder how he ever got it done."

Again we were silent, each busy with our own thoughts. I was counting up the time I give to club work and lodge work and – yes, I'll admit it – politics. My mother and my mother-in-law had none of these, and they do use up a good many hours. Instead of all this, they took time once in a while from their day and night working to go visit a neighbor for the day.

"Time to enjoy life!" Well, they did enjoy it, but it couldn't have been because they had more time.

Laura Ingalls Wilder

At Rocky Ridge in the early 1900's, working on a small farm was still very tiring and unending. When Laura was weary, she would read these Bible selections in Matthew 11 and Romans 8.

Christ said,

> Mat 11:28 ESV
> (28) Come to me, all who labor and are heavy laden, and I will give you rest.

Life can be burdensome.

All our adult lives we have to work, just to stay alive. Most people don't even like their work, but they plod on with it for forty or fifty years. The carrot that is at the end of that long stick is retirement, that period of life when people finally are free to do what they want. People obsess with their retirement plans, their 401k's and IRA's, looking forward to that idyllic time when their lives are free of the burden of making a living.

Except—

People stop working when they are old because they are old. Old means worn out, broken down, sick, frail and –

about to die.

> Ecc 12:1-7 Bible in Basic English (BBE)
> (1) Let your mind be turned to your Maker in the days of your strength, while the evil days come not, and the years are far away when you will say, I have no pleasure in them;
> (2) While the sun, or the light, or the moon, or the stars, are not dark, and the clouds come not back after the rain;
> (3) In the day when the keepers of the house are shaking for fear, and the strong men are bent down, and

the women who were crushing the grain are at rest because their number is small, and those looking out of the windows are unable to see;

(4) When the doors are shut in the street, and the sound of the crushing is low, and the voice of the bird is soft, and the daughters of music will be made low;

(5) And he is in fear of that which is high, and danger is in the road, and the tree is white with flower, and the least thing is a weight, and desire is at an end, because man goes to his last resting-place, and those who are sorrowing are in the streets;

(6) Before ever the silver cord is cut, or the vessel of gold is broken, or the pot is broken at the fountain, or the wheel broken at the water-hole;

(7) And the dust goes back to the earth as it was, and the spirit goes back to God who gave it.

Our tiring physical work gives us short term benefit, but is ultimately useless.

Ecc 2:18-23 BBE

(18) Hate had I for all my work which I had done, because the man who comes after me will have its fruits.

(19) And who is to say if that man will be wise or foolish? But he will have power over all my work which I have done and in which I have been wise under the sun. This again is to no purpose.

(20) So my mind was turned to grief for all the trouble I had taken and all my wisdom under the sun.

(21) Because there is a man whose work has been done with wisdom, with knowledge, and with an expert hand; but one who has done nothing for it will have it for his heritage. This again is to no purpose and a great evil.

(22) What does a man get for all his work, and for the

weight of care with which he has done his work under the sun?

(23) All his days are sorrow, and his work is full of grief. Even in the night his heart has no rest. This again is to no purpose.

All our lives we struggle to stay alive, fully well knowing that in the end we will lose that battle. We will die.

Many times during this lifelong scrabble, we get weary. How short sighted it is to look ahead to our retirement for relief from our weariness, when that is the time we will be most physically weary. People focus much more time on their Individual Retirement Accounts than on their Eternal Retirement Accounts.

Life has a much bigger purpose than the here and now. The here and now is just to prepare for the there and then. This life is not supposed to be heaven on earth. It is a test, a trial, a burden. The key to life is shifting that burden to the Life-giver.

> Mat 11:27-30 BBE
> (27) All things have been given to me by my Father; and no one has knowledge of the Son, but the Father; and no one has knowledge of the Father, but the Son, and he to whom the Son will make it clear.
> (28) Come to me, all you who are troubled and weighted down with care, and I will give you rest.
> (29) Take my yoke on you and become like me, for I am gentle and without pride, and you will have rest for your souls;
> (30) For my yoke is good, and the weight I take up is not hard.

That is the only way to get rid of the burden of a wearying physical life that you know will soon end, and you don't even know exactly when.

When Laura was very weary from exhausting physical farm work, she did not read these verses to look ahead to her retirement years. When she read from Romans 8, "If God is for us, who can be against us?" she wasn't looking for an easier way to hoe corn. When she read, "Who shall separate us from the love of Christ," she wasn't thinking vacation.

She read these verses to look to Christ for long term relief from her weariness: Matthew 11, shifting the burden to Him; and Romans 8, if God is for us, what difference does a little persecution, famine, peril – or weariness matter?

> Mat 11:28,30 ESV
>
> (28) Come to me, all who labor and are heavy laden, and I will give you rest.
>
> (30) For my yoke is easy, and my burden is light."
>
> Rom 8:31-39 ESV
>
> (31) What then shall we say about these things? If God is for us, who can be against us?
>
> (32) He who didn't spare his own Son, but delivered him up for us all, how would he not also with him freely give us all things?
>
> (33) Who could bring a charge against God's chosen ones? It is God who justifies.
>
> (34) Who is he who condemns? It is Christ who died, yes rather, who was raised from the dead, who is at the right hand of God, who also makes intercession for us.
>
> (35) Who shall separate us from the love of Christ? Could oppression, or anguish, or persecution, or famine, or nakedness, or peril, or sword?
>
> (36) Even as it is written, "For your sake we are killed all day long. We were accounted as sheep for the slaughter."
>
> (37) No, in all these things, we are more than conquerors through him who loved us.

(38) For I am persuaded, that neither death, nor life, nor angels, nor principalities, nor things present, nor things to come, nor powers,
(39) nor height, nor depth, nor any other created thing, will be able to separate us from the love of God, which is in Christ Jesus our Lord.

Chapter Nine

When things are going from bad to worse
2 Timothy 3d

When things are going
from bad to worse
2 Timothy 3d

II Timothy 3

2Ti 3:1-17 KJ

(1) This know also, that in the last days perilous times shall come.

(2) For men shall be lovers of their own selves, covetous, boasters, proud, blasphemers, disobedient to parents, unthankful, unholy,

(3) Without natural affection, trucebreakers, false accusers, incontinent, fierce, despisers of those that are good,

(4) Traitors, heady, highminded, lovers of pleasures more than lovers of God;

(5) Having a form of godliness, but denying the power thereof: from such turn away.

(6) For of this sort are they which creep into houses, and lead captive silly women laden with sins, led away with divers lusts,

(7) Ever learning, and never able to come to the knowledge of the truth.

(8) Now as Jannes and Jambres withstood Moses, so do these also resist the truth: men of corrupt minds, reprobate concerning the faith.

(9) But they shall proceed no further: for their folly shall be manifest unto all men, as theirs also was.

(10) But thou hast fully known my doctrine, manner of life, purpose, faith, longsuffering, charity, patience,

(11) Persecutions, afflictions, which came unto me at

Antioch, at Iconium, at Lystra; what persecutions I endured: but out of them all the Lord delivered me.

(12) Yea, and all that will live godly in Christ Jesus shall suffer persecution.

(13) But evil men and seducers shall wax worse and worse, deceiving, and being deceived.

(14) But continue thou in the things which thou hast learned and hast been assured of, knowing of whom thou hast learned them;

(15) And that from a child thou hast known the holy scriptures, which are able to make thee wise unto salvation through faith which is in Christ Jesus.

(16) All scripture is given by inspiration of God, and is profitable for doctrine, for reproof, for correction, for instruction in righteousness:

(17) That the man of God may be perfect, thoroughly furnished unto all good works.

The apostle Paul wrote this short letter to Timothy, his son in the faith. Paul mentions to Timothy in this section that "from a child thou hast known the holy scriptures, which are able to make thee wise unto salvation through faith which is in Christ Jesus."

Laura wrote of something similar in her own life.

We have been gathering the fruits of the season's work into barns and bins and cellars. The harvest has been abundant, and a good supply is stored away for future needs.

Now I am wondering what sort of fruits and how plentiful is the supply we have stored away in our hearts and souls and minds from our year's activities. The time of gathering together the visible results of our year's labor is a very appropriate time to reckon up the invisible, more important harvest...

We lay away the gleanings of our years in the edifice of our character where nothing is ever lost. What have we stored away in this safe place during the season that is past? Is it something that will keep sound and pure and sweet or something that is faulty and not worth storing?

As a child I learned my Bible lessons by heart in the good old-fashioned way, and once won the prize for repeating correctly more verses from the Bible than any other person in the Sunday school. But always my mind had a trick of picking a text here and there and connecting them together in meaning. In this way there came to me a thought that makes the stores from my invisible harvest important to me. These texts are familiar to everyone. It is their sequence that gives the thought.

Laura Ingalls Wilder

What a wonderful blessing that is for a parent to give a child the knowledge of the Word of God. There is no knowledge which is more valuable. No science, social studies, literature, or mathematics text can ever come close to the value of just one chapter of the Bible. Other texts are only the words of men. The Bible actually is the words, thoughts and plans of Almighty God.

Laura learned the Bible at home from her parents. Formerly the home was the base for religious training. Not the schools and not even the church. They all taught the Bible, but the home was the base from which right and wrong were instilled. In addition, Laura was homeschooled for part of her education, further enriching the Bible training she received, as homeschooling does today.

Paul said here that, "All scripture is given by inspiration of God, and is profitable for doctrine, for reproof, for correction, for instruction in righteousness: That the man of God may be perfect, thoroughly furnished unto all good works." For Timothy that was the Hebrew scriptures, the Old Testament. For us today that is the whole Bible.

Parents will go to great expense and make great sacrifices to get their children into the "best" universities. Yet few parents simply take the time to give their children the knowledge of the Great Creator and His Word. Ironic it is, too, that the "best" universities mock the Bible, and the God who wrote it.

How did we come to be in such a strange position in America that the one book which, more than any other, trained the minds of America's founders and early heroes is not even allowed to be taught in our schools? The Gideons can't even come into the schools to give out free Bibles.

How odd it is that someone like young Laura Ingalls, who had her head filled with Bible verses, Bible principles and Bible teachings – how odd it is that this great writer would be mocked if she went to school today. Her parents would be thought narrow minded at best, and at worst possibly dangerous. Her gift of knowing and streaming Bible verses would be laughed at and lampooned.

There is even a move among modernists to have Laura Ingalls Wilder's books banned as being harmful to children. Wouldn't she be surprised at that!

Now what was that about things going from bad to worse?

What might Laura have meant, when she said she read this chapter when things were going from bad to worse?

She might have been referring to personal relationships. Nellie Oleson comes to mind. However, Paul's statements are very broad and severe.

"This know also, that in the last days perilous times shall come. For men shall be lovers of their own selves, covetous, boasters, proud, blasphemers, disobedient to parents, unthankful, unholy, without natural affection, trucebreakers, false accusers, incontinent, fierce, despisers of those that are good, traitors, heady, highminded, lovers of pleasures more than lovers of God; having a form of godliness, but denying the power thereof: from such turn away."

Paul is talking about a major trend in society.

There is an overall progression in history.

The Age of Reason, beginning at the late seventeenth century, substituted human reason for God's revelation. It was and is thought that the human spirit can be changed with education. With enough education, humans can achieve peace and perfection.

The theory of evolution, the premise that life began without a life giver, was the result of human reason. Most of the world's thinking today is based on the premise that life did not come from God but came from nothing. If life came from nothing, there is no absolute right and wrong and no responsibility to do right and avoid wrong.

This progression of history can be easily seen in the United States. America was founded as an outwardly Christian nation. That form of Christian belief and practice was indeed not very close to that of the New Testament believers in Jerusalem, but it did acknowledge that as being good. Although the Bible might not have been most carefully followed, its teachings were acknowledged as being right and it was diligently studied by many. Although Christ may not have been closely imitated, He was accepted as the Son of God and the Savior of mankind. It was accepted that human nature itself is destructive and in need of correcting.

In the United States today, the Bible is widely viewed by the liberals as a malicious myth. Christ is said to have not even lived. And to be Christian is to be intolerant.

The Bible no longer determines right and wrong. Right and wrong is determined by each individual for himself. Selfish human nature becomes the guide, and that has led us to II Timothy 3.

What might Laura have meant, when she said she read this chapter when things were going from bad to worse?

She saw an increase in crime and general immorality, as people moved from the farms to the cities. Cities concentrate destructive human nature. Today a majority of the world population lives in an urban area. Laura saw that movement begin.

Laura also saw the World Wars. The First World War wasn't even called that until the second one came along, only one generation later. Those two wars brought human destruction to a new level never before seen in history, as man's inventiveness improved his ability to kill. Human reason and widespread education have not changed the human spirit. Indeed it has putrefied.

I think Laura was referring to a major trend, of things going from bad to worse. She saw it in the world, in the nation, and in her own family. That which was called a new morality was just old immorality.

Surely she would not have imagined where we are today, a half century after her death. Half of all families are destroyed, babies are butchered, and men marry men. The Bible is banned in the schools and Laura's books are beginning to be avoided.

That's what Paul is talking about in II Timothy 3. And here is his answer: "Continue in what you have learned and have firmly believed, knowing from whom you learned it and how from childhood you have been acquainted with the sacred writings, which are able to make you wise for salvation through faith in Christ Jesus."

That is the only answer when things are going from bad to worse, and they are.

2Ti 3:1-17 ESV
(1) But understand this, that in the last days there will come times of difficulty.
(2) For people will be lovers of self, lovers of money, proud, arrogant, abusive, disobedient to their parents, ungrateful, unholy,
(3) heartless, unappeasable, slanderous, without self-control, brutal, not loving good,
(4) treacherous, reckless, swollen with conceit, lovers of pleasure rather than lovers of God,
(5) having the appearance of godliness, but denying its power. Avoid such people.
(6) For among them are those who creep into households and capture weak women, burdened with sins and led astray by various passions,
(7) always learning and never able to arrive at a knowledge of the truth.
(8) Just as Jannes and Jambres opposed Moses, so these men also oppose the truth, men corrupted in mind and disqualified regarding the faith.
(9) But they will not get very far, for their folly will be plain to all, as was that of those two men.
(10) You, however, have followed my teaching, my conduct, my aim in life, my faith, my patience, my love, my steadfastness,
(11) my persecutions and sufferings that happened to me at Antioch, at Iconium, and at Lystra--which persecutions I endured; yet from them all the Lord rescued me.

(12) Indeed, all who desire to live a godly life in Christ Jesus will be persecuted,

(13) while evil people and impostors will go on from bad to worse, deceiving and being deceived.

(14) But as for you, continue in what you have learned and have firmly believed, knowing from whom you learned it

(15) and how from childhood you have been acquainted with the sacred writings, which are able to make you wise for salvation through faith in Christ Jesus.

(16) All Scripture is breathed out by God and profitable for teaching, for reproof, for correction, and for training in righteousness,

(17) that the man of God may be competent, equipped for every good work.

Chapter Ten

When friends
go back on you
hold to
I Corinthians 13th

When friends go back on you hold to I Corinthians 13th

I Corinthians 13

1Co 13:1-13 KJ

(1) Though I speak with the tongues of men and of angels, and have not charity, I am become as sounding brass, or a tinkling cymbal.

(2) And though I have the gift of prophecy, and understand all mysteries, and all knowledge; and though I have all faith, so that I could remove mountains, and have not charity, I am nothing.

(3) And though I bestow all my goods to feed the poor, and though I give my body to be burned, and have not charity, it profiteth me nothing.

(4) Charity suffereth long, and is kind; charity envieth not; charity vaunteth not itself, is not puffed up,

(5) Doth not behave itself unseemly, seeketh not her own, is not easily provoked, thinketh no evil;

(6) Rejoiceth not in iniquity, but rejoiceth in the truth;

(7) Beareth all things, believeth all things, hopeth all things, endureth all things.

(8) Charity never faileth: but whether there be prophecies, they shall fail; whether there be tongues, they shall cease; whether there be knowledge, it shall vanish away.

(9) For we know in part, and we prophesy in part.

(10) But when that which is perfect is come, then that which is in part shall be done away.

(11) When I was a child, I spake as a child, I understood as a child, I thought as a child: but when I became a man, I put away childish things.

(12) For now we see through a glass, darkly; but then face to face: now I know in part; but then shall I know even as also I am known.

(13) And now abideth faith, hope, charity, these three; but the greatest of these is charity.

I Corinthians 13 is known as the love chapter. The Greek word which is translated as "charity" in the King James Version is agape, meaning affection, benevolence or love. Most other translations render the word as love, as charity today means giving alms. This chapter is accepted as being one of the greatest portions of the Bible, in beauty of meaning and language.

The Corinthian Christians or Christianos were mostly Gentiles, and they acted like it. They still had all sorts of un-Christlike behavior, including fighting with each other.

1Co 6:1-8 ESV

(1) When one of you has a grievance against another, does he dare go to law before the unrighteous instead of the saints?

(2) Or do you not know that the saints will judge the world? And if the world is to be judged by you, are you incompetent to try trivial cases?

(3) Do you not know that we are to judge angels? How much more, then, matters pertaining to this life!

(4) So if you have such cases, why do you lay them before those who have no standing in the church?

(5) I say this to your shame. Can it be that there is no one among you wise enough to settle a dispute between the brothers,

(6) but brother goes to law against brother, and that before unbelievers?

(7) To have lawsuits at all with one another is already a defeat for you. Why not rather suffer wrong? Why not rather be defrauded?

(8) But you yourselves wrong and defraud--even your own brothers!

It wasn't enough that they had persecution from the Jews and Romans. They also persecuted each other.

At the end of chapter 12, Paul said that he would show them a more excellent way. I Corinthians 13 is it.

Love is putting the other person first, even when they do you wrong.

> Mat 5:38-48 ESV
> (38) "You have heard that it was said, 'An eye for an eye and a tooth for a tooth.'
> (39) But I say to you, Do not resist the one who is evil. But if anyone slaps you on the right cheek, turn to him the other also.
> (40) And if anyone would sue you and take your tunic, let him have your cloak as well.
> (41) And if anyone forces you to go one mile, go with him two miles.
> (42) Give to the one who begs from you, and do not refuse the one who would borrow from you.
> (43) "You have heard that it was said, 'You shall love your neighbor and hate your enemy.'
> (44) But I say to you, Love your enemies and pray for those who persecute you,
> (45) so that you may be sons of your Father who is in heaven. For he makes his sun rise on the evil and on the good, and sends rain on the just and on the unjust.
> (46) For if you love those who love you, what reward do you have? Do not even the tax collectors do the same?

(47) And if you greet only your brothers, what more are you doing than others? Do not even the Gentiles do the same?

(48) You therefore must be perfect, as your heavenly Father is perfect.

That's what Laura was talking about when she said, "When friends go back on you hold to I Corinthians 13th."

She tried to be kind to her dear friends.

> *In my glance backward and hope for the future, one thing became plain to me – that I valued the love and appreciation of my friends more than ever before, and that I would try to show my love for them, that I would be more careful of their feelings, more tactful, and so endear myself to them.*
>
> *Laura Ingalls Wilder*

So Laura took in the love chapter. What did that do in her life? What effect did that have?

Have you ever thought about how unhappy the Little House books really are?

Think about it.

In 1863 Pa Ingalls bought a farm in the big woods of Wisconsin, cleared some land, built a log house and raised crops. Mary and Laura were born there. Grandpas and grandmas and aunts and uncles and cousins lived close by. *Little House in the Big Woods* tells about that. But – Pa wanted to leave the little log house, the big woods and all the relatives and move. Life might be easier somewhere else.

In 1868 he sold his Wisconsin farm and bought a farm in Missouri. That episode is not in any of the Little House books.

The next year they left Missouri and moved to Kansas, trying to set up a homestead on an Indian reservation. *Little House on the Prairie* tells that story. Carrie was born there.

In 1871 the Ingalls moved back to their old place in Wisconsin, taking the farm back from the buyer when he gave up on it. Pa sold the farm again and they moved in with his parents for the winter.

In 1874 they moved to Walnut Grove, Minnesota. There they bought a farm and lived by a creek in a hole in the ground, a dug out, until Pa got a new house built. *On the Banks of Plum Creek* tells of that.

In 1876 Pa sold his Plum Creek farm and moved in with his brother in Minnesota. Laura's only little brother died there.

Later that year the family moved to Burr Oak, Iowa. Grace was born there.

In 1878 the Ingalls moved back to Walnut Grove, Minnesota. Pa didn't buy a farm but built a house in another man's pasture. Mary caught scarlet fever there and lost her eyesight.

In 1879 Pa went to work for the railroad. The family moved to De Smet, Dakota Territory, which became South Dakota. *On the Shores of Silver Lake* tells how they spent the first winter in Dakota in the surveyors' house.

Pa filed a claim on a homestead and built a tarpaper covered shanty on the land. He also built a building in the new little town of De Smet, which their family lived in during *The Long Winter* of 1880-81. *Those Happy Golden Years* tells of living near De Smet, as Ma may have prevailed on Pa to finally quit moving. Laura got married in De Smet in 1885 when she was 18.

What a deprived, unfortunate life that was.

Laura lived in thirteen homes in her first thirteen years of life: Wisconsin, Missouri, Kansas, Wisconsin, Ingalls' parents, Walnut Grove, Pa's brother in Minnesota, Iowa, Walnut Grove, surveyors' house, homestead shanty, house in town, and back to homestead shanty.

Pa had a problem. It was the old green grass and fence problem.

Laura lived in thirteen homes, lost a baby brother, her big sister went blind – what an unhappy existence!

And that unhappy life is told in the Little House books.

But wait – the Little House books are not unhappy. They are some of the happiest books you will ever read. They jump with jollity!

What happened?

Laura applied the love chapter.

Laura wrote with love when she was writing her books. For example, the way she viewed her parents. Were her parents perfect? Far from it. All the moves, living in tarpapered shacks, even living in a hole in the ground. If Laura's parents raised her today the way she was actually raised, the state bureaucracy would take her and her poor sisters away from their parents. Living in a hole in the ground like rats!

Did Laura resent her parents for that upbringing?

Absolutely not! When you read the Little House books, you might think that Laura's parents were nearly perfect. They obviously weren't. But Laura viewed her parents through the love of Christ in the love chapter: she suffered long, and was kind.

In Laura's books, there is no rancor. There is only good will. The books have a pleasant spirit. Think about this scene, repeated over and over in her books. The family is together on a cold night, and they are fed and full and the fire is warm and flickering. Pa is playing his frolicking fiddle, while Ma and the girls are sitting together enjoying the music and the warmth.

You can see that scene, can't you? What is that? That is love in the living room! Or parlor. Or shanty.

There are no kids bawling and brawling. There is no pouting and shouting. There is only love. Love flickers in the firelight. Love fancies with the fiddle. Love fills the room, as it is shared by the family.

Laura's books are an example of what happens when you write with your mind full of I Corinthians 13.

Do you want your family to be like that?

Then write your life as an extension of the love chapter.

Laura applied I Cor 13 when she wrote her stories. If there is one thing that makes her books have such wide appeal, it is the love that she stroked with her pencil.

The only possible exception to that might be Nellie Oleson, but hey! –

She was Nellie Oleson!

> 1Co 13:1-13 BBE
> (1) If I make use of the tongues of men and of angels, and have not love, I am like sounding brass, or a loud-tongued bell.
> (2) And if I have a prophet's power, and have knowledge of all secret things; and if I have all faith, by which mountains may be moved from their place, but

have not love, I am nothing.

(3) And if I give all my goods to the poor, and if I give my body to be burned, but have not love, it is of no profit to me.

(4) Love is never tired of waiting; love is kind; love has no envy; love has no high opinion of itself, love has no pride;

(5) Love's ways are ever fair, it takes no thought for itself; it is not quickly made angry, it takes no account of evil;

(6) It takes no pleasure in wrongdoing, but has joy in what is true;

(7) Love has the power of undergoing all things, having faith in all things, hoping all things.

(8) Though the prophet's word may come to an end, tongues come to nothing, and knowledge have no more value, love has no end.

(9) For our knowledge is only in part, and the prophet's word gives only a part of what is true:

(10) But when that which is complete is come, then that which is in part will be no longer necessary.

(11) When I was a child, I made use of a child's language, I had a child's feelings and a child's thoughts: now that I am a man, I have put away he things of a child.

(12) For now we see things in a glass, darkly; but then face to face: now my knowledge is in part; then it will be complete, even as God's knowledge of me.

(13) But now we still have faith, hope, love, these three; and the greatest of these is love.

Chapter Eleven

For inward peace
the 14th chapter of
St. John

For inward peace
the 14th chapter of St. John

John 14

Joh 14:1-31 KJ

(1) Let not your heart be troubled: ye believe in God, believe also in me.

(2) In my Father's house are many mansions: if it were not so, I would have told you. I go to prepare a place for you.

(3) And if I go and prepare a place for you, I will come again, and receive you unto myself; that where I am, there ye may be also.

(4) And whither I go ye know, and the way ye know.

(5) Thomas saith unto him, Lord, we know not whither thou goest; and how can we know the way?

(6) Jesus saith unto him, I am the way, the truth, and the life: no man cometh unto the Father, but by me.

(7) If ye had known me, ye should have known my Father also: and from henceforth ye know him, and have seen him.

(8) Philip saith unto him, Lord, shew us the Father, and it sufficeth us.

(9) Jesus saith unto him, Have I been so long time with you, and yet hast thou not known me, Philip? he that hath seen me hath seen the Father; and how sayest thou then, Shew us the Father?

(10) Believest thou not that I am in the Father, and the Father in me? the words that I speak unto you I speak

not of myself: but the Father that dwelleth in me, he doeth the works.

(11) Believe me that I am in the Father, and the Father in me: or else believe me for the very works' sake.

(12) Verily, verily, I say unto you, He that believeth on me, the works that I do shall he do also; and greater works than these shall he do; because I go unto my Father.

(13) And whatsoever ye shall ask in my name, that will I do, that the Father may be glorified in the Son.

(14) If ye shall ask any thing in my name, I will do it.

(15) If ye love me, keep my commandments.

(16) And I will pray the Father, and he shall give you another Comforter, that he may abide with you for ever;

(17) Even the Spirit of truth; whom the world cannot receive, because it seeth him not, neither knoweth him: but ye know him; for he dwelleth with you, and shall be in you.

(18) I will not leave you comfortless: I will come to you.

(19) Yet a little while, and the world seeth me no more; but ye see me: because I live, ye shall live also.

(20) At that day ye shall know that I am in my Father, and ye in me, and I in you.

(21) He that hath my commandments, and keepeth them, he it is that loveth me: and he that loveth me shall be loved of my Father, and I will love him, and will manifest myself to him.

(22) Judas saith unto him, not Iscariot, Lord, how is it that thou wilt manifest thyself unto us, and not unto the world?

(23) Jesus answered and said unto him, If a man love me, he will keep my words: and my Father will love him, and we will come unto him, and make our abode with him.

(24) He that loveth me not keepeth not my sayings: and

the word which ye hear is not mine, but the Father's which sent me.

(25) These things have I spoken unto you, being yet present with you.

(26) But the Comforter, which is the Holy Ghost, whom the Father will send in my name, he shall teach you all things, and bring all things to your remembrance, whatsoever I have said unto you.

(27) Peace I leave with you, my peace I give unto you: not as the world giveth, give I unto you. Let not your heart be troubled, neither let it be afraid.

(28) Ye have heard how I said unto you, I go away, and come again unto you. If ye loved me, ye would rejoice, because I said, I go unto the Father: for my Father is greater than I.

(29) And now I have told you before it come to pass, that, when it is come to pass, ye might believe.

(30) Hereafter I will not talk much with you: for the prince of this world cometh, and hath nothing in me.

(31) But that the world may know that I love the Father; and as the Father gave me commandment, even so I do. Arise, let us go hence.

For inward peace the 14th chapter of St. John, Laura said.

We do not think of Laura as needing to find inward peace. Some homes are routinely in an uproar. Laura always lived in a peaceful home, both the Ingalls' and then her own.

Laura loved living in the country, and she found peace from that, as most people do. One of the hidden benefits of being a farmer's wife is living in the peaceful country.

There seems to be a madness in the cities, a frenzy in the struggling crowds. A friend writes me of New York "I like it and I hate it. There's something you've got to love, it's so big – a people hurrying everywhere, all, trying to live and be someone or something -- and then, when you see the poverty and hatefulness, the uselessness of it all, you wonder why people live there at all. It does not seem possible that there are any peaceful farms on earth."

And so more than ever I am thankful for the peacefulness and comparative isolation of country life. This is a happiness which we ought to realize and enjoy.

Laura Ingalls Wilder

Laura lived in the country, but still found a need for inward peace. What would have caused that? When might that have been?

Perhaps the prime cause of distress for people is their children. That stress might be caused by a child conflicting with the parent, by a child's behavior, or by a child's health. Laura only had two children, but she had all those causes of upset.

Surely one of the times when Laura most needed inner peace was when her son died. Surely, also, there is no pain like losing a child. He was born normally in August of 1889, before the doctor made it to the house, even. Twelve days later Laura was back on her feet and working normally when the little boy was taken with spasms, as she described it. He died before a doctor could get to him.

Laura described the time after that as being blurred. She described herself as being numb.

She wrote about that in the book *The First Four Years*. That is a rough draft manuscript which was found after Laura's death. It is not a work of art as the Little House books are. It was just put away and left, unfinished.

Nava Austin was the librarian in Mansfield when Laura used to come there often after Manly had died. I asked Nava why Laura didn't continue the series farther.

> *Editor: Why didn't she write more books? She had quite a number of years left to write about, if she had wanted to.*
>
> *Nava: She just didn't want to write about the sad things. The first years of their marriage were rough, and she thought that was too sad to write about.*
>
> From *Laura Ingalls' Friends Remember Her,* by Dan L. White

Laura must have written *The First Four Years* after her last Little House book, *These Happy Golden Years,* was published in 1943. If Laura wrote it down that year, she would have been seventy-six years old. She was twenty-one when her little boy died. At least fifty-five years had passed since her baby's death. Fifty-five years – a long time. Yet when Laura wrote about it in *The First Four Years,* she only talked about it for two short paragraphs. Two paragraphs and fifty-five words, one word for every year that had passed.

And then she stuck that writing away and never finished it.

Did she need inner peace when she was twenty-one, and for long afterwards?

I think so.

There is no pain for a parent like losing a child. The parent would rather lose herself than lose her child, but she can't make that trade.

In John 14, the Messiah is most concerned with comforting His followers.

At the end of the previous chapter, Christ had just washed the disciples' feet. He who had never sinned cleaned the dirt off the feet of filthy sinners.

He had given them bread and wine, which pictured his body being beaten and his blood poured out. That was going to happen the very next day.

And he had told Peter that the daring disciple would be so timid and faithless that he would deny Christ three times before the rooster rared back to announce the next sunrise a few hours away.

After all that, knowing all the suffering that He will be facing, He tells them not to be troubled.

Before He suffers, before He is denied by His own, before He is mocked by the priesthood He had set up, before He is killed by those He came to save –

He takes time to encourage those who are around Him. "Don't let your heart be troubled."

What consideration.

Consideration is love in action. That was some action.

Laura said she read John 14 for inward peace. In this chapter Christ says:

- Let not your hearts be troubled.
- Peace I leave with you; my peace I give to you.
- Let not your hearts be troubled, neither let them be afraid.

Twice here Christ tells them to not let their hearts be troubled. This in the face of the terrible trouble that was upon Him and them that day.

Why was He not troubled?

He was the one directly facing arrest, mocking, beating and bleeding. Normally when someone faces execution, others try to comfort him. Particularly when the one being executed has done no deed to deserve his fate, and may have difficulty understanding why that which is happening to him is happening. Yet Christ is comforting the disciples.

Having done no sin, and being hung up like the greatest sinner, the Messiah was not troubled, and He could tell them not to be troubled.

Why?

Because He knew the end at the beginning.

Before He was taken to die, He knew that He would live. Before His blood was poured out of Him, He could see the spirit being poured back into Him. Before His seamless robe was gambled off, He could see His head covering folded on the rock shelf in His tomb. Before He went to Golgotha, the site of the execution, He could see Himself going to the throne of God.

The earliest church observed the Passover festival. Three centuries later there was a dispute over when to observe this, on the original day on the 14th of the month or on the Sunday following the 14th, when it was said that Christ was resurrected. At the Passover, the resurrection was guaranteed. Once the Messiah had died in the faith, that faith would raise Him again. There was no doubt, no question, no possibility that would not be so. At that Passover, the resurrection was absolute.

Christ tells His disciples not to be troubled, because they can have the same faith, the same spirit, the same future. They can know the end at the beginning. "My peace I give to you."

Joh 14:1-31 ESV
"Let not your hearts be troubled. Believe in God; believe also in me.

In my Father's house are many rooms. If it were not so, would I have told you that I go to prepare a place for you? And if I go and prepare a place for you, I will come again and will take you to myself, that where I am you may be also. And you know the way to where I am going."

Thomas said to him, "Lord, we do not know where you are going. How can we know the way?"

Jesus said to him, "I am the way, and the truth, and the life. No one comes to the Father except through me. If you had known me, you would have known my Father also. From now on you do know him and have seen him."

Philip said to him, "Lord, show us the Father, and it is enough for us."

Jesus said to him, "Have I been with you so long, and you still do not know me, Philip? Whoever has seen me has seen the Father. How can you say, 'Show us the Father'? Do you not believe that I am in the Father and the Father is in me?

The words that I say to you I do not speak on my own authority, but the Father who dwells in me does his works. Believe me that I am in the Father and the Father is in me, or else believe on account of the works themselves. Truly, truly, I say to you, whoever believes in me will also do the works that I do; and greater works than these will he do, because I am going to the Father. Whatever you ask in my name, this I will do, that the Father may be glorified in the Son. If you ask me anything in my name, I will do it.

If you love me, you will keep my commandments. And I will ask the Father, and he will give you another Helper, to be with you forever, even the Spirit of truth, whom the world cannot receive, because it neither sees him nor knows him. You know him, for he dwells with you and will be in you.

I will not leave you as orphans; I will come to you. Yet a little while and the world will see me no more, but you will see me. Because I live, you also will live. In that day you will know that I am in my Father, and you in me, and I in you.

Whoever has my commandments and keeps them, he it is who loves me. And he who loves me will be loved by my Father, and I will love him and manifest myself to him.

Judas (not Iscariot) said to him, "Lord, how is it that you will manifest yourself to us, and not to the world?"

Jesus answered him, "If anyone loves me, he will keep my word, and my Father will love him, and we will come to him and make our home with him. Whoever does not love me does not keep my words. And the word that you hear is not mine but the Father's who sent me.

These things I have spoken to you while I am still with you. But the Helper, the Holy Spirit, whom the Father will send in my name, he will teach you all things and bring to your remembrance all that I have said to you.

Peace I leave with you; my peace I give to you. Not as the world gives do I give to you. Let not your hearts be troubled, neither let them be afraid.

You heard me say to you, 'I am going away, and I will come to you.' If you loved me, you would have rejoiced, because I am going to the Father, for the Father is greater than I. And now I have told you before it takes place, so that when it does take place you may believe.

I will no longer talk much with you, for the ruler of this world is coming. He has no claim on me, but I do as the Father has commanded me, so that the world may know that I love the Father. Rise, let us go from here.

Chapter Twelve

To avoid misfortune
Matthew 7:24 to 27

Matthew 27:24 - 27

Mat 7:24-27 KJ
(24) Therefore whosoever heareth these sayings of mine, and doeth them, I will liken him unto a wise man, which built his house upon a rock:
(25) And the rain descended, and the floods came, and the winds blew, and beat upon that house; and it fell not: for it was founded upon a rock.
(26) And every one that heareth these sayings of mine, and doeth them not, shall be likened unto a foolish man, which built his house upon the sand:
(27) And the rain descended, and the floods came, and the winds blew, and beat upon that house; and it fell: and great was the fall of it.

Laura and Manly Wilder moved from South Dakota to near Mansfield, Missouri in 1894. They bought 40 acres a mile east of Mansfield, mostly wooded, with a log cabin and a thousand young apple trees.

When Laura and Manly came to the Ozarks, they had to make a living from that 40 acres of rocky land, which they named Rocky Ridge Farm. To make it, they had to have a plan, a solid base. On the way to the Ozarks, they had met wagons and wagons of people who were leaving, who had not made it. In fact, the 40 acres they bought had been given up on by the previous owner. He had bought the apple trees to set out on the place, stuck their roots in a ditch to keep them alive, and then just given up.

Laura and Manly faced a tremendous challenge trying to live off their little farm. We have lived in the Ozarks for years, about a dozen miles from Laura's farm. The topsoil here is very much on top but very little soil, only a couple of inches deep on the hills, and that two inches is scattered with rocks. When they bought their forty acres, Manly said that the open field was worn out from being over cropped, and the poor land wouldn't grow a stalk of corn over four feet tall. In fact, Manly did not even want to buy the place.

They arrived in the Ozarks at the end of the summer and used what money they had to pay on the farm. To live through the winter, they cut firewood to sell. Wood will always sell, at some price. Cutting wood is extremely hard work, even today with power tools. Back then the tool was a long two man saw and the power had to come from the shoulder and the arm.

Laura helped Manly cut wood that first winter. Half Pint was half the sawing team, each pushing back at the other from the end of the two man saw. Or more accurately, pulling. They cleared the land to make room to plant the apple trees, they used the wood for their own heat, and they sold the wood. Others in the area also cut wood, holding the price down. The first cord of wood that Almanzo sold brought only fifty cents. But most people didn't cut wood to sell, because the work was just too demanding.

The next spring Laura and Manly put out a garden to get much of their food. They began to add animals, like chickens – they had brought a few with them from De Smet -- and a cow. The chickens gave eggs and meat. The cow gave milk and meat from a calf raised to butcher. They also set out the apple trees on the land they had cleared, but it took years for them to start bearing.

After that first winter, making a living did not get easy for the Wilders. They made progress at Rocky Ridge, but it was slow.

Sometimes Manly took other jobs, in addition to farming, such as selling kerosene or driving a dray, which was a type of hauling wagon. Even 21 years later, Laura and Manly were still scrabbling just to stay ahead. When Laura visited Rose in San Francisco in 1915, they still had a $500 mortgage on Rocky Ridge Farm, which was more than they had paid for it to begin with. It seems they might have taken a mortgage to loan some money to Rose and her husband Gillette, which Gillette had trouble repaying.

However, through all their work and through all the years, Laura and Manly always had Rocky Ridge Farm. No matter how bad times got, they always had that 40 acres to live on and live from. That could supply their food, their fuel and their shelter. Laura even discussed a plan which described in detail how to make a living on a few acres. They had done it.

In the Great Depression of the 1930's, people who lived in the cities and lost their jobs had to stand in lines at soup kitchens to get something to eat. People who lived on farms were usually somewhat better off. Although they might not have been able to get much money, at least they could get food from their farm, although a part of the country during the depression was in a drought.

Most people today don't have a piece of land as their economic base. Families today don't have homeplaces or family farms, and they would never think of having a name for their home. They don't have a Rocky Ridge.

Rocky Ridge was not a base of sand. It was a base of rock – literally, with a little top soil. Rocky Ridge Farm was the rock on which Laura and Manly based their economy. It wasn't great land, but it was their land, and if they took care of it, it took care of them. Whatever economic misfortune befell them, they could live from their little farm.

Of course, the Rock on which a person should base his life is Christ.

He said, "Whoever hears these sayings of mine ..." What sayings?

The ones He had just made.

> Mat 7:13-23 ESV
> (13) "Enter by the narrow gate. For the gate is wide and the way is easy that leads to destruction, and those who enter by it are many.
> (14) For the gate is narrow and the way is hard that leads to life, and those who find it are few.
> (15) "Beware of false prophets, who come to you in sheep's clothing but inwardly are ravenous wolves.
> (16) You will recognize them by their fruits. Are grapes gathered from thornbushes, or figs from thistles?
> (17) So, every healthy tree bears good fruit, but the diseased tree bears bad fruit.
> (18) A healthy tree cannot bear bad fruit, nor can a diseased tree bear good fruit.
> (19) Every tree that does not bear good fruit is cut down and thrown into the fire.
> (20) Thus you will recognize them by their fruits.
> (21) "Not everyone who says to me, 'Lord, Lord,' will enter the kingdom of heaven, but the one who does the will of my Father who is in heaven.
> (22) On that day many will say to me, 'Lord, Lord, did we not prophesy in your name, and cast out demons in your name, and do many mighty works in your name?'
> (23) And then will I declare to them, 'I never knew you; depart from me, you workers of lawlessness.'

Whoever hears these sayings builds his house on a rock. In these sayings Christ is talking about obedience.

He said to enter at the narrow gate. The broad road leads to destruction, and most will take that road. Very few will take the road which leads to life.

Christ is viewed by the world as being tolerant of any sin they commit. When Christians stand against sin, it is said that they are not being like Christ – that they are not being tolerant. The world says that because they do not know the Bible and they do not know the Messiah. They only know the broad way, the popular opinion, which indulges any and all sins and hates rebuke.

All groups, all churches and all people are swayed by society to whatever degree. Some a little. Most a lot. Christ alone is the Rock on which we must base our belief. He alone is the standard, perfect and unchanging. His words are the greatest words ever written in the history of mankind. He must be our main focus: not a church, a group, or a person, but only the Son of God.

America is sliding downhill on a slope of sin. Almost everybody is comfortable with that. Most keep sliding along, and few try to stand against the flow. Everybody looks at everybody else, and if they are all going the same way, it must be all right. Christians must get back to looking beyond people to perfection: to Him who said, "Be ye therefore perfect, even as your Father in heaven is perfect." We must look to the perfect Messiah as our standard.

> 1Co 10:1-4 ESV
> (1) For I want you to know, brothers, that our fathers were all under the cloud, and all passed through the sea,
> (2) and all were baptized into Moses in the cloud and in the sea,
> (3) and all ate the same spiritual food,

(4) and all drank the same spiritual drink. For they drank from the spiritual Rock that followed them, and the Rock was Christ.

For everyone, that spiritual Rock is Christ.

> Mat 7:24-27 ESV
> (24) "Everyone then who hears these words of mine and does them will be like a wise man who built his house on the rock.
> (25) And the rain fell, and the floods came, and the winds blew and beat on that house, but it did not fall, because it had been founded on the rock.
> (26) And everyone who hears these words of mine and does not do them will be like a foolish man who built his house on the sand.
> (27) And the rain fell, and the floods came, and the winds blew and beat against that house, and it fell, and great was the fall of it."

Chapter Thirteen

For record of what trust in God can do, Hebrews 11

Hebrews 11

Heb 11:1-40 KJ
(1) Now faith is the substance of things hoped for, the evidence of things not seen.
(2) For by it the elders obtained a good report.
(3) Through faith we understand that the worlds were framed by the word of God, so that things which are seen were not made of things which do appear.
(4) By faith Abel offered unto God a more excellent sacrifice than Cain, by which he obtained witness that he was righteous, God testifying of his gifts: and by it he being dead yet speaketh.
(5) By faith Enoch was translated that he should not see death; and was not found, because God had translated him: for before his translation he had this testimony, that he pleased God.
(6) But without faith it is impossible to please him: for he that cometh to God must believe that he is, and that he is a rewarder of them that diligently seek him.
(7) By faith Noah, being warned of God of things not seen as yet, moved with fear, prepared an ark to the saving of his house; by the which he condemned the world, and became heir of the righteousness which is by faith.
(8) By faith Abraham, when he was called to go out into a place which he should after receive for an

inheritance, obeyed; and he went out, not knowing whither he went.

(9) By faith he sojourned in the land of promise, as in a strange country, dwelling in tabernacles with Isaac and Jacob, the heirs with him of the same promise:

(10) For he looked for a city which hath foundations, whose builder and maker is God.

(11) Through faith also Sara herself received strength to conceive seed, and was delivered of a child when she was past age, because she judged him faithful who had promised.

(12) Therefore sprang there even of one, and him as good as dead, so many as the stars of the sky in multitude, and as the sand which is by the sea shore innumerable.

(13) These all died in faith, not having received the promises, but having seen them afar off, and were persuaded of them, and embraced them, and confessed that they were strangers and pilgrims on the earth.

(14) For they that say such things declare plainly that they seek a country.

(15) And truly, if they had been mindful of that country from whence they came out, they might have had opportunity to have returned.

(16) But now they desire a better country, that is, an heavenly: wherefore God is not ashamed to be called their God: for he hath prepared for them a city.

(17) By faith Abraham, when he was tried, offered up Isaac: and he that had received the promises offered up his only begotten son,

(18) Of whom it was said, That in Isaac shall thy seed be called:

(19) Accounting that God was able to raise him up, even from the dead; from whence also he received him in a figure.

(20) By faith Isaac blessed Jacob and Esau concerning things to come.

(21) By faith Jacob, when he was a dying, blessed both the sons of Joseph; and worshipped, leaning upon the top of his staff.

(22) By faith Joseph, when he died, made mention of the departing of the children of Israel; and gave commandment concerning his bones.

(23) By faith Moses, when he was born, was hid three months of his parents, because they saw he was a proper child; and they were not afraid of the king's commandment.

(24) By faith Moses, when he was come to years, refused to be called the son of Pharaoh's daughter;

(25) Choosing rather to suffer affliction with the people of God, than to enjoy the pleasures of sin for a season;

(26) Esteeming the reproach of Christ greater riches than the treasures in Egypt: for he had respect unto the recompence of the reward.

(27) By faith he forsook Egypt, not fearing the wrath of the king: for he endured, as seeing him who is invisible.

(28) Through faith he kept the passover, and the sprinkling of blood, lest he that destroyed the firstborn should touch them.

(29) By faith they passed through the Red sea as by dry land: which the Egyptians assaying to do were drowned.

(30) By faith the walls of Jericho fell down, after they were compassed about seven days.

(31) By faith the harlot Rahab perished not with them that believed not, when she had received the spies with peace.

(32) And what shall I more say? for the time would fail me to tell of Gedeon, and of Barak, and of Samson, and of Jephthae; of David also, and Samuel, and of the prophets:

(33) Who through faith subdued kingdoms, wrought righteousness, obtained promises, stopped the mouths of lions,

(34) Quenched the violence of fire, escaped the edge of the sword, out of weakness were made strong, waxed valiant in fight, turned to flight the armies of the aliens.

(35) Women received their dead raised to life again: and others were tortured, not accepting deliverance; that they might obtain a better resurrection:

(36) And others had trial of cruel mockings and scourgings, yea, moreover of bonds and imprisonment:

(37) They were stoned, they were sawn asunder, were tempted, were slain with the sword: they wandered about in sheepskins and goatskins; being destitute, afflicted, tormented;

(38) (Of whom the world was not worthy:) they wandered in deserts, and in mountains, and in dens and caves of the earth.

(39) And these all, having obtained a good report through faith, received not the promise:

(40) God having provided some better thing for us, that they without us should not be made perfect.

Farmers trust in God. They have to. They depend on the seed, the sunshine and the rain. God created those and He controls the laws which cause them to do what they do. Even if a farmer doesn't believe in God, he still depends on God for his farming.

The season is over, the rush and struggle of growing and saving the crops is past for another year, and the time has come when we pause and reverently give thanks for the harvest. For it is not to our efforts alone that our measure of success is due, but to the life principle in the earth and the seed, to the sunshine, and to the rain – to the goodness of God.

We may not be altogether satisfied with the year's results, and we can do a terrific amount of grumbling when we take the notion. But I am sure we all know in our hearts that we have a great deal for which to be thankful. In spite of disappointment and weariness and perhaps sorrow, His goodness and mercy does follow us all the days of our lives.

Laura Ingalls Wilder

When Manly asked Laura to marry him, she told him she didn't want to marry a farmer. They agreed to try farming for three years. If they were not successful in that time, Manly would try something else.

But those first three years were marked both by destructive storms and drought. Laura gave him a fourth year, a year of grace, to see if they could make it at farming.

At the end of that year, things were hardly better. However, Laura had changed her view of living on and from the land. Even if the crops hadn't made, they still thought they would make it.

"Now faith is the substance of things hoped for, the evidence of things not seen," Hebrews 11:1, KJ.

That's what a farmer does. He has faith. That which is hoped for and not seen is this year's crop. The farmer has the seemingly absurd position of taking a small seed and instead of eating it, hides it in the ground. He knows that it will rot, but he hopes that buried seed will regenerate itself a hundred times over.

That position is logically absurd because that happens in only one place in the whole universe – earth.

The sun is just the right distance from the earth to give the right amount of heat. The atmosphere of the earth is just right to let the perfect amount of sunlight through. The water vapor is in a perpetual cycle, going from the oceans into the air, then floating over the farmer's field and dropping summer showers.

The nitrogen is in an endless cycle. It is in the air and is transferred to the ground by lightning and plants. Then some bacteria fixate that nitrogen, making it available to fertilize plants. Animals eat those plants and take that nitrogen into their bodies. Then they die and decay, and other bacteria put the nitrogen back into the air again.

How convenient.

All of these complex processes, and many more, operate continuously, all interconnected in a marvelous maze of magnificence. Scientists have calculated that there is absolutely no mathematical chance of all of this just happening.

Sometimes it is said that farmers, or people who grow their own food, are self-sufficient. They're not. They're God dependent.

Farmers work with God's creation, probably more than any other profession. As human society has gotten more mechanized, people have gotten farther away from seeing the creation on a daily basis. Most people live in urban and suburban megalopolises and have to make special trips just to see nature. Because of that, most people today are less aware of the natural laws of creation, and hardly think at all of the force behind those laws, which is Almighty God. When people go from the country to the city, they change.

Farmers work with God's creation, and they have the opportunity to learn more about Him. Most of all, they have the opportunity to learn faith. "Without faith it is impossible to please him, for whoever would draw near to God must believe that he exists and that he rewards those who seek him," Hebrews 11:6.

One who chooses to truly follow Christ is like that little seed that the farmer hides in the ground. He gives up this life, just as the farmer gives up eating his seed. He eventually dies and expires, just as the seed rots, without ever seeing his main goal in life, the Kingdom of God. But just as the seed is powerfully regenerated, so the Christ follower will be renewed like an eight foot corn stalk, in the harvest to come.

To give up this life for the life to come requires faith. Just as Christ had when He did that.

>Heb 11:1-40 ESV
>(1) Now faith is the assurance of things hoped for, the conviction of things not seen.
>(2) For by it the people of old received their commendation.
>(3) By faith we understand that the universe was created by the word of God, so that what is seen was not made out of things that are visible.
>(4) By faith Abel offered to God a more acceptable sacrifice than Cain, through which he was commended as righteous, God commending him by accepting his gifts. And through his faith, though he died, he still speaks.
>(5) By faith Enoch was taken up so that he should not see death, and he was not found, because God had taken him. Now before he was taken he was commended as having pleased God.
>(6) And without faith it is impossible to please him, for whoever would draw near to God must believe that he exists and that he rewards those who seek him.
>(7) By faith Noah, being warned by God concerning events as yet unseen, in reverent fear constructed an ark for the saving of his household. By this he condemned the world and became an heir of the righteousness that comes by faith.
>(8) By faith Abraham obeyed when he was called to go out to a place that he was to receive as an inheritance. And he went out, not knowing where he was going.

(9) By faith he went to live in the land of promise, as in a foreign land, living in tents with Isaac and Jacob, heirs with him of the same promise.

(10) For he was looking forward to the city that has foundations, whose designer and builder is God.

(11) By faith Sarah herself received power to conceive, even when she was past the age, since she considered him faithful who had promised.

(12) Therefore from one man, and him as good as dead, were born descendants as many as the stars of heaven and as many as the innumerable grains of sand by the seashore.

(13) These all died in faith, not having received the things promised, but having seen them and greeted them from afar, and having acknowledged that they were strangers and exiles on the earth.

(14) For people who speak thus make it clear that they are seeking a homeland.

(15) If they had been thinking of that land from which they had gone out, they would have had opportunity to return.

(16) But as it is, they desire a better country, that is, a heavenly one. Therefore God is not ashamed to be called their God, for he has prepared for them a city.

(17) By faith Abraham, when he was tested, offered up Isaac, and he who had received the promises was in the act of offering up his only son,

(18) of whom it was said, "Through Isaac shall your offspring be named."

(19) He considered that God was able even to raise him from the dead, from which, figuratively speaking, he did receive him back.

(20) By faith Isaac invoked future blessings on Jacob and Esau.

(21) By faith Jacob, when dying, blessed each of the sons of Joseph, bowing in worship over the head of his staff.

(22) By faith Joseph, at the end of his life, made mention of the exodus of the Israelites and gave directions concerning his bones.

(23) By faith Moses, when he was born, was hidden for three months by his parents, because they saw that the child was beautiful, and they were not afraid of the king's edict.

(24) By faith Moses, when he was grown up, refused to be called the son of Pharaoh's daughter,

(25) choosing rather to be mistreated with the people of God than to enjoy the fleeting pleasures of sin.

(26) He considered the reproach of Christ greater wealth than the treasures of Egypt, for he was looking to the reward.

(27) By faith he left Egypt, not being afraid of the anger of the king, for he endured as seeing him who is invisible.

(28) By faith he kept the Passover and sprinkled the blood, so that the Destroyer of the firstborn might not touch them.

(29) By faith the people crossed the Red Sea as on dry land, but the Egyptians, when they attempted to do the same, were drowned.

(30) By faith the walls of Jericho fell down after they had been encircled for seven days.

(31) By faith Rahab the prostitute did not perish with those who were disobedient, because she had given a friendly welcome to the spies.

(32) And what more shall I say? For time would fail me to tell of Gideon, Barak, Samson, Jephthah, of David and Samuel and the prophets--

(33) who through faith conquered kingdoms, enforced justice, obtained promises, stopped the mouths of lions,

(34) quenched the power of fire, escaped the edge of the sword, were made strong out of weakness, became mighty in war, put foreign armies to flight.

(35) Women received back their dead by resurrection. Some were tortured, refusing to accept release, so that they might rise again to a better life.

(36) Others suffered mocking and flogging, and even chains and imprisonment.

(37) They were stoned, they were sawn in two, they were killed with the sword. They went about in skins of sheep and goats, destitute, afflicted, mistreated--

(38) of whom the world was not worthy--wandering about in deserts and mountains, and in dens and caves of the earth.

(39) And all these, though commended through their faith, did not receive what was promised,

(40) since God had provided something better for us, that apart from us they should not be made perfect.

Chapter Fourteen

If you are having to put up a fight, the end of Ephesians

If you are having to put up a fight,
the end of Ephesians

Ephesians 6:10 - 18

Eph 6:10-18 KJ

(10) Finally, my brethren, be strong in the Lord, and in the power of his might.

(11) Put on the whole armour of God, that ye may be able to stand against the wiles of the devil.

(12) For we wrestle not against flesh and blood, but against principalities, against powers, against the rulers of the darkness of this world, against spiritual wickedness in high places.

(13) Wherefore take unto you the whole armour of God, that ye may be able to withstand in the evil day, and having done all, to stand.

(14) Stand therefore, having your loins girt about with truth, and having on the breastplate of righteousness;

(15) And your feet shod with the preparation of the gospel of peace;

(16) Above all, taking the shield of faith, wherewith ye shall be able to quench all the fiery darts of the wicked.

(17) And take the helmet of salvation, and the sword of the Spirit, which is the word of God:

(18) Praying always with all prayer and supplication in the Spirit, and watching thereunto with all perseverance and supplication for all saints;

The apostle Paul in this section tells us to put on the armor of God, so that we may stand against the wiles of the devil.

Laura said to read this section if you are having to put up a fight. Ultimately that fight is against the wiles of the devil.

Paul said that we don't wrestle against flesh and blood, but against spiritual wickedness in high places. That spiritual wickedness can show itself in ourselves and in others.

Laura wrote this about encountering it in others.

> *Mrs. A was angry. Her eyes snapped, her voice was shrill, and a red flag of rage was flying upon each cheek. She expected opposition and anger at the things she said, but her remarks were answered in a soft voice; her angry eyes were met by smiling ones; and her attack was smothered in the softness of courtesy, consideration, and compromise.*
>
> *I feel sure Mrs. A had intended to create a disturbance, but she might as well have tried to break a feather pillow by beating it as to have any effect with her angry voice and manner on the perfect kindness and good manners which met her. She only made herself ridiculous, and in self-defense was obliged to change her attitude.*
>
> *Since then I have been wondering if it always is so, if shafts of malice aimed in anger forever fall harmless against the armor of a smile, kind words, and gentle manners. I believe they do. And I have gained a fuller understanding of the words, "A soft answer turneth away wrath" (Prov. 15:1).*
>
> *Until this incident, I had found no more in the words than the idea that a soft answer might cool the wrath of an aggressor, but I saw wrath turned away as an arrow deflected from its mark and came to understand that a soft answer and a courteous manner are an actual protection.*

Nothing is ever gained by allowing anger to have sway. While under its influence, we lose the ability to think clearly and lose the forceful power that is in calmness.

Anger is a destructive force; its purpose is to hurt and destroy, and being a blind passion, it does its evil work, not only upon whatever arouses it, but also upon the person who harbors it. Even physically it injures him, impeding the action of the heart and circulation, affecting the respiration, and creating an actual poison in the blood. Persons with weak hearts have been known to drop dead from it, and always there is a feeling of illness after indulging in a fit of temper.

Anger is a destroying force. What all the world needs is its opposite – an uplifting power.

Laura Ingalls Wilder

In this example, the armor of God was the word of God – a soft answer turns away wrath. The one being attacked was armed with the gospel of peace.

Actually the one being attacked may have been Laura herself. As she wrote these personal reflections for her magazine articles, she drew from her everyday experiences. Of course, she could not bluntly say that she was the one who turned away wrath with a soft answer, but that may indeed have been the case, unless she was an awkward bystander in such an encounter by others.

Laura herself was known to be vulnerable to the wiles of the devil in letting loose a sharp, tempestuous tongue.

Anna Gutschke lived near Mansfield and knew Laura and Rose. We interviewed her for the book *Laura Ingalls' Friends Remember Her*. The Wilder family shared Thanksgiving dinner for several years with the Gutschkes.

Anna was asked, "Some people have described Mrs. Wilder as being quiet and reserved. What was she like to you?"

Anna answered bluntly, "She was strict and had strong opinions. She had a temper and it flared."

Daughter Rose sometimes described her mother's responses as snapping or flaring.

Pa Ingalls had once warned Laura about that tendency. At the beginning of the book *These Happy Golden Years*, he told her that she sometimes spoke and acted too quickly. Laura had remembered that lesson from Pa, and doubtless spent a lifetime trying to learn it.

At times, though, in standing against the wiles of the devil, it is necessary to speak out against what others are doing.

In Ephesians, Paul went on to say:

> Eph 6:18-20 KJ
> (18) praying at all times in the Spirit, with all prayer and supplication. To that end keep alert with all perseverance, making supplication for all the saints,
> (19) and also for me, that words may be given to me in opening my mouth boldly to proclaim the mystery of the gospel,
> (20) for which I am an ambassador in chains, that I may declare it boldly, as I ought to speak.

Paul asked that they pray for him, that he might open his mouth boldly. Yet for his bold speaking, he was a prisoner.

Why was he in prison, since he preached the gospel of peace?

He was in prison because he stood up for what was right, and therefore had to stand against what was wrong.

That is the fight.

When people stand for wrong, it is wrong not to speak out against that. But when you do, you must make sure that you speak not from yourself, but from the gospel of peace, wearing the belt of truth, carrying the shield of faith, with the sword of the spirit, the Word of God.

What America lacks today is people who are willing to put up that fight. She lacks people who have the boldness of Paul, who spoke the gospel of peace and was persecuted for it.

It is not just morals which are under attack in America – it is Christ Himself who is being attacked. They say He never lived at all, and is not even a historical figure. Or they say He was not born of a virgin, and that He was an adulterer Himself. Or they say He was not the Son of God, but a charlatan out for a glory trip.

Most of all, they say He is not the one way to life, as He said He is. "I am the way, the truth, and the life," John 14:6. Thus they call Him, who died for them, a liar.

Christians need to fight against that, with the gospel of peace and the sword of the spirit.

When you have to put up a fight, read the end of Ephesians.

> Eph 6:10-18 ESV
> (10) Finally, be strong in the Lord and in the strength of his might.
> (11) Put on the whole armor of God, that you may be able to stand against the schemes of the devil.
> (12) For we do not wrestle against flesh and blood, but against the rulers, against the authorities, against the cosmic powers over this present darkness, against the spiritual forces of evil in the heavenly places.

(13) Therefore take up the whole armor of God, that you may be able to withstand in the evil day, and having done all, to stand firm.

(14) Stand therefore, having fastened on the belt of truth, and having put on the breastplate of righteousness,

 (15) and, as shoes for your feet, having put on the readiness given by the gospel of peace.

(16) In all circumstances take up the shield of faith, with which you can extinguish all the flaming darts of the evil one;

(17) and take the helmet of salvation, and the sword of the Spirit, which is the word of God,

(18) praying at all times in the Spirit, with all prayer and supplication. To that end keep alert with all perseverance, making supplication for all the saints.

Chapter Fifteen

When you have sinned read I John 3, 1 to 21

When you have sinned read
I John 3, 1 to 21

I John 3:1- 21

1Jn 3:1-21 KJ

(1) Behold, what manner of love the Father hath bestowed upon us, that we should be called the sons of God: therefore the world knoweth us not, because it knew him not.

(2) Beloved, now are we the sons of God, and it doth not yet appear what we shall be: but we know that, when he shall appear, we shall be like him; for we shall see him as he is.

(3) And every man that hath this hope in him purifieth himself, even as he is pure.

(4) Whosoever committeth sin transgresseth also the law: for sin is the transgression of the law.

(5) And ye know that he was manifested to take away our sins; and in him is no sin.

(6) Whosoever abideth in him sinneth not: whosoever sinneth hath not seen him, neither known him.

(7) Little children, let no man deceive you: he that doeth righteousness is righteous, even as he is righteous.

(8) He that committeth sin is of the devil; for the devil sinneth from the beginning. For this purpose the Son of God was manifested, that he might destroy the works of the devil.

(9) Whosoever is born of God doth not commit sin; for his seed remaineth in him: and he cannot sin, because he is born of God.

(10) In this the children of God are manifest, and the children of the devil: whosoever doeth not righteousness is not of God, neither he that loveth not his brother.

(11) For this is the message that ye heard from the beginning, that we should love one another.

(12) Not as Cain, who was of that wicked one, and slew his brother. And wherefore slew he him? Because his own works were evil, and his brother's righteous.

(13) Marvel not, my brethren, if the world hate you.

(14) We know that we have passed from death unto life, because we love the brethren. He that loveth not his brother abideth in death.

(15) Whosoever hateth his brother is a murderer: and ye know that no murderer hath eternal life abiding in him.

(16) Hereby perceive we the love of God, because he laid down his life for us: and we ought to lay down our lives for the brethren.

(17) But whoso hath this world's good, and seeth his brother have need, and shutteth up his bowels of compassion from him, how dwelleth the love of God in him?

(18) My little children, let us not love in word, neither in tongue; but in deed and in truth.

(19) And hereby we know that we are of the truth, and shall assure our hearts before him.

(20) For if our heart condemn us, God is greater than our heart, and knoweth all things.

(21) Beloved, if our heart condemn us not, then have we confidence toward God.

Laura wrote about a couple of incidents where she was afraid she had given offense to some of her friends.

> *A friend and I went together to an afternoon gathering where refreshments were served, and we came back to my friend's home just as the evening meal was ready.*

The Man of the Place had failed to meet me and so I stayed unexpectedly. My friend made apologies for the simple meal, and I said that I preferred plain food to such as we had in the afternoon, which was the same as saying that her meal was plain and that the afternoon refreshments had been finer. I felt that I had said the wrong thing, and in a desperate effort to make amends, I praised the soup which had been served. Not being satisfied to let well enough alone, because of my embarrassment I continued, "It is so easy to have delicious soups, one can make them of just any little things that are left."

And all the way home as I rode quietly beside the Man of the Place I kept praying "The Fool's Prayer": "O Lord, be merciful to me, a fool."

We can afford to laugh at a little mistake such as that, however embarrassing it may be. To laugh and forget is one of the saving graces, but only a little later I was guilty of another mistake over which I could not laugh.

Mrs. G and I were in a group of women at a social affair; but having a little business to talk over, we stepped into another room where we were almost immediately followed by an acquaintance. We greeted her and then went on with our conversation, from which she was excluded. I forgot her presence, and then I looked her way again; she was gone. We had not been kind, and to make it worse, she was comparatively a stranger among us.

In a few minutes everyone was leaving without my having had a chance to make amends in any way. I could not apologize without giving a point to the rudeness, but I thought that I would be especially gracious to her when we met again so she would not feel that we made her an outsider. Now I learn that it will be months before I see her again. I know that she is very sensitive and that I must have hurt her. Again and from the bottom of my heart, I prayed "The Fool's Prayer":

These clumsy feet, still in the mire,
Go crushing blossoms without end;
These hard, well-meaning hands we thrust
Among the heart strings of a friend –
O Lord, be merciful to me, a fool.

Laura Ingalls Wilder

It would seem that since Laura was so concerned over leaving a friend out of a conversation, that almost surely meant that she customarily avoided the great sins to which people often succumb. And that comes from having your head filled with the Bible, as she did. When you do sin, you know what sin is, you know you shouldn't do it, and you can repent.

Laura said to read I John 3 when you have sinned. This was written by John who was the bosom buddy of Christ. Christ never sinned. He died for our sins. He gives us His same spirit to help us overcome sin. Yet John wrote this letter to early Christians who apparently believed it was all right to sin.

Notice what John said:

- Purifies himself, as He is pure.
- Sin is the transgression of the law.
- He came to take away sin.
- No one who lives in Him keeps on sinning.
- Don't be deceived. He who practices righteousness is righteous.
- Whoever practices sin is of the devil.
- No one of God makes a practice of sinning.

Also notice verse 22, which Laura did not include. –

> 1Jn 3:22 KJ
> (22) And whatsoever we ask, we receive of him, because we keep his commandments, and do those things that are pleasing in his sight.

This letter of John, Christ's bosom buddy, is a strong admonition not to sin.

Of course, most people's sins extend far beyond just leaving someone out of a conversation. Of itself, the human spirit can't help but sin. The carnal or natural mind is God's enemy.

> Rom 8:7 KJ
> (7) Because the carnal mind is enmity against God: for it is not subject to the law of God, neither indeed can be.

Humanism teaches that the human spirit is basically good, just lacking in enough education. God says that the human spirit is wicked, and lacking His spirit.

> Jer 17:9 KJ
> (9) The heart is deceitful above all things, and desperately wicked: who can know it?

All have sinned, except for the Son of God. Even studies of old Puritan wedding dates and first child birth dates come up short of nine months quite often. Isn't that surprising? Well, not too much. They had that same carnal nature.

Today America is losing its knowledge of what sin is.

Up until recently in the United States, when people committed sins such as sexual sins, they acknowledged it as such. They had done wrong, but they knew and admitted that it was wrong, because the Bible told them that. Since the nation had a general knowledge of the Bible, that society tended to point people to a higher level of behavior, even when they weren't particularly religious.

Today that society is no more. Now evil is called good, and good is called evil. Those who teach and spread sin are admired, and those few who stand against sin are castigated.

> Isa 5:20 KJ
> (20) Woe unto them that call evil good, and good evil; that put darkness for light, and light for darkness; that put bitter for sweet, and sweet for bitter!

> Jer 4:22 KJ
> (22) For my people is foolish, they have not known me; they are sottish children, and they have none understanding: they are wise to do evil, but to do good they have no knowledge.

> Mal 2:17 KJ
> (17) Ye have wearied the LORD with your words. Yet ye say, Wherein have we wearied him? When ye say, Every one that doeth evil is good in the sight of the LORD, and he delighteth in them; or, Where is the God of judgment?

If a young lady became pregnant before marriage in Puritan times, they knew that was sin. Usually the young man involved married the young lady as quickly as could be arranged. Less than nine months later, a baby arrived. Premature, no doubt, but full size. They did not flaunt the sin. And almost always the child had a family to grow up in.

Today in America about one in three babies is born out of family. There is no attempt to hide this sin, which is a crime against God and children. Couples live together without marrying, with no hint of shame. The most sordid kind of sexual behaviors are committed by people all over the land, and they are proud of it and have pornographic parades to promote it.

In all of this, there is no admission that this perversity is sin, a breaking of God's law, the Ten Commandments. If America does not know what sin is, America cannot know how to repent.

The apostle John faced the very same situation when he wrote this short letter. Christians were practicing sin and saying that was good. John wrote this little letter to straighten them out.

He told them what sin is – the transgression of God's law – and then he told them not to do it.

1Jn 3:1-21 ESV

(1) See what kind of love the Father has given to us, that we should be called children of God; and so we are. The reason why the world does not know us is that it did not know him.
(2) Beloved, we are God's children now, and what we will be has not yet appeared; but we know that when he appears we shall be like him, because we shall see him as he is.
(3) And everyone who thus hopes in him purifies himself as he is pure.
(4) Everyone who makes a practice of sinning also practices lawlessness; sin is lawlessness.
(5) You know that he appeared to take away sins, and in him there is no sin.
(6) No one who abides in him keeps on sinning; no one who keeps on sinning has either seen him or known him.

(7) Little children, let no one deceive you. Whoever practices righteousness is righteous, as he is righteous.

(8) Whoever makes a practice of sinning is of the devil, for the devil has been sinning from the beginning. The reason the Son of God appeared was to destroy the works of the devil.

(9) No one born of God makes a practice of sinning, for God's seed abides in him, and he cannot keep on sinning because he has been born of God.

(10) By this it is evident who are the children of God, and who are the children of the devil: whoever does not practice righteousness is not of God, nor is the one who does not love his brother.

(11) For this is the message that you have heard from the beginning, that we should love one another.

(12) We should not be like Cain, who was of the evil one and murdered his brother. And why did he murder him? Because his own deeds were evil and his brother's righteous.

(13) Do not be surprised, brothers, that the world hates you.

(14) We know that we have passed out of death into life, because we love the brothers. Whoever does not love abides in death.

(15) Everyone who hates his brother is a murderer, and you know that no murderer has eternal life abiding in him.

(16) By this we know love, that he laid down his life for us, and we ought to lay down our lives for the brothers.

(17) But if anyone has the world's goods and sees his brother in need, yet closes his heart against him, how does God's love abide in him?

(18) Little children, let us not love in word or talk but in deed and in truth.

(19) By this we shall know that we are of the truth and reassure our heart before him;

(20) for whenever our heart condemns us, God is greater than our heart, and he knows everything.

(21) Beloved, if our heart does not condemn us, we have confidence before God.

Chapter Sixteen

And make Psalm 51 your prayer

And make Psalm 51 your prayer

Psalm 51

Psa 51:1-19 KJ

To the chief Musician, A Psalm of David, when Nathan the prophet came unto him, after he had gone in to Bathsheba.

(1) Have mercy upon me, O God, according to thy lovingkindness: according unto the multitude of thy tender mercies blot out my transgressions.

(2) Wash me throughly from mine iniquity, and cleanse me from my sin.

(3) For I acknowledge my transgressions: and my sin is ever before me.

(4) Against thee, thee only, have I sinned, and done this evil in thy sight: that thou mightest be justified when thou speakest, and be clear when thou judgest.

(5) Behold, I was shapen in iniquity; and in sin did my mother conceive me.

(6) Behold, thou desirest truth in the inward parts: and in the hidden part thou shalt make me to know wisdom.

(7) Purge me with hyssop, and I shall be clean: wash me, and I shall be whiter than snow.

(8) Make me to hear joy and gladness; that the bones which thou hast broken may rejoice.

(9) Hide thy face from my sins, and blot out all mine iniquities.

(10) Create in me a clean heart, O God; and renew a right spirit within me.

(11) Cast me not away from thy presence; and take not thy holy spirit from me.

(12) Restore unto me the joy of thy salvation; and uphold me with thy free spirit.

(13) Then will I teach transgressors thy ways; and sinners shall be converted unto thee.

(14) Deliver me from bloodguiltiness, O God, thou God of my salvation: and my tongue shall sing aloud of thy righteousness.

(15) O Lord, open thou my lips; and my mouth shall shew forth thy praise.

(16) For thou desirest not sacrifice; else would I give it: thou delightest not in burnt offering.

(17) The sacrifices of God are a broken spirit: a broken and a contrite heart, O God, thou wilt not despise.

(18) Do good in thy good pleasure unto Zion: build thou the walls of Jerusalem.

(19) Then shalt thou be pleased with the sacrifices of righteousness, with burnt offering and whole burnt offering: then shall they offer bullocks upon thine altar.

The great mistake of youth is to underestimate the challenge of life.

When Manly and Laura began farming, he was quite confident. Laura had not wanted to marry a farmer, so Manly told her to give him three years. He was confident that he would be successful at farming within three years and Laura would be glad she had married a well to do farmer.

At that time, in the 1880's, people could get a homestead from the government if only they could live on it and make it a working farm. It was said that the government bet 160 acres that you couldn't survive on it. Confident Manly took out a claim not on one homestead, but two, a regular homestead and a tree claim on which he had to plant and keep alive ten acres of trees. Trees did not grow there naturally, so that meant they didn't want to.

Here is what happened during their first three years together, the years when they were going to be successful at farming.

Right after they got married at the end of August, Manly harvested a wheat crop that was surprisingly poor, only ten bushels to the acre. Besides that, the prices were low, only ten cents per bushel. Normally when yields are down prices are up. Manly caught the low side of the deal both ways.

That first year they took on some debt, for tools and provisions. The debt could be paid off with a good crop.

The next summer Manly planted a hundred acres of wheat. Rains came and the crop grew wonderfully well. Manly decided the wheat was ready to harvest and went in debt to buy a binder to harvest it. He cut a little of it but decided to wait a couple more days, until the wheat was just perfect. Late that afternoon a twenty minute hailstorm destroyed the wheat crop.

The next summer the wheat harvest was low again.

The next winter Laura and Manly caught diphtheria. Manly was permanently impaired.

The next summer the wheat crop was good. Before it was harvested, a three day hot wind cooked the wheat and made it worthless except for hay. That ended the three year trial for farming.

Laura gave Manly a fourth year.

In the fourth year the ten acres of trees on the tree claim died from the hot, dry weather. They had a baby son. He died twelve days later. Soon after that their house burned, destroying most of their homemaking possessions. Finally they gave up on their homesteads.

What would Manly and Laura have learned from all that?

Humility. To repent of arrogance and self confidence, and to place their confidence somewhere else.

> *The Man of the Place was worried about the weather. He said the indications were for a dry season, and ever since I have been remembering droughts. There were dry years in the Dakotas when we were beginning our life together. How heartbreaking it was to watch the grain we had sown with such high hopes wither and turn yellow in the hot winds! And it was backbreaking as well as heartbreaking to carry water from the well to my garden and see it dry up despite all my efforts.*
>
> *I said at that time that thereafter I would sow the seed, but the Lord would give the increase if there was any, for I could not do my work and that of Providence also by sending the rain on the gardens of the just or the unjust.*
>
> *Laura Ingalls Wilder*

Psalm 51 is the ultimate song of repentance and humility. It is so movingly sad to think of King David

- who had beaten Goliath with God and a slingshot;
- who had refused to lift a hand against King Saul, when Saul was trying to kill him, because Saul was Yahweh's anointed;
- who had united all Israel behind him, and under God;
- who had sung songs from his heart to Yahweh while watching sheep, with no one else to hear other than the sheep and God Himself –

This King David fell to the level of a common slut. The guy who wrote "Yahweh is my shepherd, I shall not want," wanted somebody else's wife. He had wives of his own, yet he happened to see another woman who was bathing, and he reached out and slurped her up like a hog in the slop.

To hide his ignominy, he multiplied his sin by killing her husband. He was loyal Uriah, one of David's most valiant thirty soldiers. David mercilessly had Joab order Uriah to go up to the wall they were attacking, where he was sure to be killed. Noble, valiant, loyal Uriah went and was.

David had not planned his great sins. They just belched out of him, like a spoiled supper. They erupted from his corrupt human nature, which saw, wanted and took. His love of self overpowered his love of Uriah, Bathsheba, and God. At that time, He was like Satan in the flesh.

Then he was told his sin, and he was smitten. Unlike Saul, who never really repented when he sinned, David saw his sin and hated it. In spite of his repentance, Yahweh gave David the punishment of never having the sword depart from his house. That was a severe and lifelong chastisement.

Years later, David's beloved son Absalom, who was more like Saul than like David, surely caused David to remember his great sins with Bathsheba and Uriah. Absalom led a conspiracy to dethrone his own father. David had to flee Jerusalem for his life, being usurped by a favorite son. Whereas David went in to Uriah's wife in secret, Absalom took David's concubines into his tent openly.

When David was rushing out of Jerusalem, fleeing for his life from his own son, an incident happened which indicates that David was thinking back to the sin which brought the sword on his house.

> 2Sa 16:5-11 WEB
> (5) When king David came to Bahurim, behold, a man of the family of the house of Saul came out, whose

name was Shimei, the son of Gera. He came out, and cursed still as he came.

(6) He cast stones at David, and at all the servants of king David: and all the people and all the mighty men were on his right hand and on his left.

(7) Thus said Shimei when he cursed, Be gone, be gone, you man of blood, and base fellow:

(8) Yahweh has returned on you all the blood of the house of Saul, in whose place you have reigned; and Yahweh has delivered the kingdom into the hand of Absalom your son; and behold, you are caught by your own mischief, because you are a man of blood.

(9) Then said Abishai the son of Zeruiah to the king, "Why should this dead dog curse my lord the king? Please let me go over and take off his head."

(10) The king said, What have I to do with you, you sons of Zeruiah? Because he curses, and because Yahweh has said to him, Curse David; who then shall say, Why have you done so?

(11) David said to Abishai, and to all his servants, Behold, my son, who came forth from my bowels, seeks my life: how much more may this Benjamite now do it? let him alone, and let him curse; for Yahweh has invited him.

The rebellion failed and Absalom was killed. David tried to avoid that, and specifically ordered Joab and his men not to harm Absalom. But the promise from God was that the sword would not depart from David's house.

Absalom had overgrown hair, just as he had an overgrown ego. While he was trying to escape from Joab, his hair got caught in a tree. How many soldiers have been captured because their hair got caught in a tree? Not many, but Absalom was. Hanging by his lovely hair from a tree, Absalom was killed by Joab. The sword had struck David's house again.

That was a severe punishment. However, David was so humbled in Psalm 51 that he did not resent his punishment. "Against you, you only, have I sinned and done what is evil in your sight, so that you may be justified in your words and blameless in your judgment." David did not pout and he did not argue against the sentence he received. He said that God was blameless in His judgment. Remember that the usual penalty for adultery was immediate stoning.

Psalm 51 is the ultimate song of repentance. Look at what David said of himself.

- according to your abundant mercy blot out my transgressions;
- wash me thoroughly from my iniquity, and cleanse me from my sin!
- my sin is ever before me;
- in sin did my mother conceive me;
- create in me a clean heart, O God, and renew a right spirit within me.

True repentance comes from true humility. True humility comes from seeing one's true position with respect to God. Job finally did. And in Psalm 51, David did. In contrast to the day he stole Bathsheba, he had a broken spirit and a humble heart.

"The sacrifices of God are a broken spirit; a broken and contrite heart, O God, you will not despise."

Growth can come from humility. Nine years after they were married, Laura and Manly came to the Ozarks. Manly still wanted to be a farmer, he still thought that was the best life, and Laura still gave him more years to do that. He passed away at Rocky Ridge in 1949, with his beloved Laura at his side, at the full old age of ninety-two. She passed on eight years later in 1957, shortly after turning ninety. She had been at Rocky Ridge Farm for sixty-three years.

The two farmers both lived past ninety. Manly had been right.

Psa 51:1-19 ESV

(1) Have mercy on me, O God, according to your steadfast love; according to your abundant mercy blot out my transgressions.

(2) Wash me thoroughly from my iniquity, and cleanse me from my sin!

(3) For I know my transgressions, and my sin is ever before me.

(4) Against you, you only, have I sinned and done what is evil in your sight, so that you may be justified in your words and blameless in your judgment.

(5) Behold, I was brought forth in iniquity, and in sin did my mother conceive me.

(6) Behold, you delight in truth in the inward being, and you teach me wisdom in the secret heart.

(7) Purge me with hyssop, and I shall be clean; wash me, and I shall be whiter than snow.

(8) Let me hear joy and gladness; let the bones that you have broken rejoice.

(9) Hide your face from my sins, and blot out all my iniquities.

(10) Create in me a clean heart, O God, and renew a right spirit within me.

(11) Cast me not away from your presence, and take not your Holy Spirit from me.

(12) Restore to me the joy of your salvation, and uphold me with a willing spirit.

(13) Then I will teach transgressors your ways, and sinners will return to you.

(14) Deliver me from bloodguiltiness, O God, O God of my salvation, and my tongue will sing aloud of your righteousness.

(15) O Lord, open my lips, and my mouth will declare your praise.

(16) For you will not delight in sacrifice, or I would give it; you will not be pleased with a burnt offering.

(17) The sacrifices of God are a broken spirit; a broken and contrite heart, O God, you will not despise.

(18) Do good to Zion in your good pleasure; build up the walls of Jerusalem;

(19) then will you delight in right sacrifices, in burnt offerings and whole burnt offerings; then bulls will be offered on your altar.

Other books by Dan L. White

Information available at danlwhitebooks.com
Email at mail@danlwhitebooks.com.
Find us on Facebook at Dan L White Books.

The Jubilee Principle: God's Plan for Economic Freedom
WND Books, available at wndbooks.com.

–examines the economic "long wave", a boom-and-bust cycle that happens roughly twice a century in free economies, and parallels the wisdom of the fifty-year Jubilee cycle in the Bible. *The Jubilee Principle* shows how God designed Israel's society with the Sabbath, festivals, land sabbath and Jubilee year. How would it be to live a whole life under that system? *The Jubilee Principle* points the way to true security.

Laura's Love Story
The lifetime love of Laura Ingalls and Almanzo Wilder

Real love is sometimes stronger than the romance of fiction. Laura and Almanzo's love is such a story. From an unwanted beau – Almanzo – to a beautiful romance; from the heart wrenching tragedy of losing their home and little boy to heartfelt passion; from trials that most do not endure to a love that endured for a lifetime –

Laura's Love Story is the true account of two young people who lived through the most trying troubles to form the most lasting love.

Better than fiction, truer than life, this is the love story that put the jollity in Laura's stories and is the final happy ending to her Little House® books.

The Long, Hard Winter of 1880-81 – What was it Really Like?

Laura Ingalls Wilder's classic novel *The Long Winter* tells the riveting story of the winter of 1880-81. She wrote of three day blizzards, forty ton trains stuck in the snow, houses buried in snowdrifts and a town that nearly starved.

Just how much of her story was fact, and how much was fiction? Was that winter really that bad, or was it just a typical old time winter stretched a bit to make a good tale?

Author Dan L. White examines the reality of the long, hard winter. Was Laura's story just fiction, or was that one winter stranger than fiction?

Laura Ingalls' Friends Remember Her
Memories from Laura's Ozark Home

– contains memories from Laura and Almanzo's close friends, Ozarkers who knew them around their home town of Mansfield, Missouri. We chat with these folks, down home and close up, about their good friends Laura and Almanzo.

Laura also joins in our chats because we include long swatches of her magazine writings on whatever subject is at hand. It's almost as if she's there talking with us. Her thoughts on family and little farms and what-not are more interesting than almost anybody you've ever talked to.

Plus the book contains discussions of –
- how Laura's Ozark life made her happy books possible;
- what made Laura's books so happy;
- whether her daughter Rose wrote Laura's books;
- and Laura's last, lonely little house.

Laura Ingalls' Friends Remember Her includes –
- her friends' recollections;
- Laura's writings from her magazine articles;
- and fresh discussions of Laura's happy books and her life.

Laura's readers should find these insights into the Little House life interesting and uplifting.

Big Bible Lessons from Laura Ingalls' Little Books

The Little House® books by Laura Ingalls Wilder are lovable, classic works of literature. They contain no violence and no vulgarities, yet they captivate young readers and whole families with their warmth and interest.

They tell the life of young Laura Ingalls, who grew up on the American frontier after the Civil War. Laura was part of a conservative Christian family, and they lived their lives based on certain unchanging values – drawn from the Bible.

Big Bible Lessons from Laura Ingalls' Little Books examines the Bible principles that are the foundation of Laura's writing, the Ingalls family, and the Little House® books. Not directly stated in words, they were firmly declared in the everyday lives of the Ingalls family. While you enjoy Laura's wonderful books, this book and these Bible lessons will help you and your family also grow spiritually from them.

Reading along with Laura Ingalls in the Big Wisconsin Woods

Little House in the Big Woods fans can now enjoy that beloved story a little more.

Reading along with Laura Ingalls in the Big Wisconsin Woods delves a little deeper into Pa's stories about panthers and bears and honey bee trees, the dance at Grandpa's house, going into the town of Pepin, and the other goings-on in Laura's book.

Read along and discover how Laura wrote her book and how the times were, in and beyond the Ingalls' cabin. Most of all, you can join in the warmth and wonderful family life that is tenderly talked about in Laura's book and in this book.

Reading along with Laura Ingalls at her Kansas Prairie Home

Little House on the Prairie is the most famous of all the great books by Laura Ingalls Wilder. There she tells how her family traveled to Kansas and built a log house, how Pa almost died digging a well, how they were almost burned out by a prairie wildfire, and how they faced possible attack from wolves and Indians.

Reading Along with Laura Ingalls at her Kansas Prairie Home goes along with that book, chapter by chapter, event by event –

and tells more about how it really was – there in 1870 on that Kansas prairie.

Little House on the Prairie deserves more than just a quick read. Such a beloved book stirs thought, reflection and remembering. *Reading Along with Laura Ingalls at her Kansas Prairie Home* does that. Read along with Laura, laugh along with Laura, live along with Laura as we search out the times and spirit of these hardy pioneers. Join in as we stretch out your enjoyment of Laura's book, deepen your understanding of her character, and increase your affection for her wonderful family.

"Oh Charles!"

The Real Laura Ingalls:
Who was Real, What was Real on her Prairie TV Show

Fans of the **Little House on the Prairie** *TV show know it was taken from Laura Ingalls Wilder's books. They know those books told the real story of Laura's life. But most have never read her books. Then they wonder —*

What really happened? Who was real? Who wasn't?

What stories on the show were like the stories in her books?

This book tells you just that.

The Real Laura Ingalls is for those fans of the show who have never read Laura's books and want to know how the show's stories connect with Laura's real life.

They do connect! From Almanzo to Nellie Oleson to sister Mary, the connection between the show's stories and Laura's stories is a fascinating story in itself. The Real Laura Ingalls tells this story in a fast moving, easy reading, crystal clear style, while upholding the values of the show and the books.

Laura Ingalls Wilder's Most Inspiring Writings
Notes and Setting by Dan L. White

*These sparkling works of Laura Ingalls Wilder came **before** she wrote her famous book Little House on the Prairie, from which the television show came. The eight other books she wrote tell of her life as a girl on the American frontier between about 1870 and 1889. But years before writing these books, she wrote articles about small farms, country living and just living life for the Missouri Ruralist magazine. Laura Ingalls Wilder's Most Inspiring Writings is a collection of forty-eight of the most interesting and uplifting of these writings.*

Within Laura's words are gems of down to earth wisdom. Amazingly, most of her comments mean just as much today as when she wrote them. These writings give us her philosophy of life and are the seed stock of Laura's prairie books.

Homeschool Happenings, Happenstance & Happiness:
A Light Look at Homeschool Life

Homeschool pioneers Margie and Dan White reflect on their homeschool experiences from 1976 until today. With *Homeschool Helpers,* they have held hundreds of homeschool activities and have put out a quarter million words of encouragement. This book includes the top tenth of those writings, everything from homeschooling in the world today to unforgettable family episodes.

Such as:

"Most people do not see themselves as part of history. If you are a Christian homeschool family, you are part of one of the great religious movements in the history of America, perhaps the greatest. Just as God put the Jews back in the Holy Land, just as He is drawing some Jews to follow Christ, so He is calling you to follow the Messiah directly."

"With no institutions supporting it, and all of them opposing it, why in the world did homeschooling grow by perhaps 20% a year?"

This book is about family, faith and fun – Homeschool happenings, happenstance, and happiness!

Tebows' Homeschooled! Should You?
How homeschooling put God back in education!

Tim Tebow is the world's most famous modern day homeschooler. His parents, Pam and Bob Tebow, homeschooled all five of their children. The intense attention on Tim has also put a spotlight on homeschooling. Although practically everyone in the country now knows about homeschooling, the movement still educates only a few percent of the overall student population. Most people are far more familiar with the factory approach to education than this method of individual tutoring.

Tim Tebow's homeschool education was typical of homeschooling in a number of ways. In some ways, of course, his experience was unique. Yet even in that uniqueness he typifies homeschooling, because homeschooling excels with uniqueness. Therefore, there is much to learn about homeschooling in general by looking at Tim Tebow's homeschooling. In this book, we try to draw out those lessons.

School Baals:
How an Old Idol with a New Name Sneaked into Your School

If you believe in the God of the Bible, that is religion and can't be taught in the government schools. If you don't believe in the God of the Bible, that is not religion and can be taught in the government schools. That is also one of the biggest deceptions ever foisted on any people in all of human history.

Idolatry is not just the worship of an idol, but the exalting of the human spirit against its creator. The same human nature that built Baal and made Molech created the anti-God deception that is taught to nine out of ten young people in America.

School Baals reveals this idolatry in all its duplicity and destruction, and tells you what you can do about it.

Life Lessons from Jane Austen's Pride and Prejudice:
From her book, her characters and her Bible

Seven characters in *Pride and Prejudice* –

> Mr. George Wickham, with a most pleasing appearance;
> Miss Jane Bennet, who thought ill of no one and who spoke against no ills;
> Miss Charlotte Lucas, who married for position and got only what she sought;
> Mr. William Collins, whose humble abode was so very close to Rosings Park;
> Miss Elizabeth Bennet, with her consuming search for a man of character;
> and Mr. Fitzwilliam Darcy, who helped her find him –

These seven characters in *Pride and Prejudice* present seven aspects of human nature and the consequent complications of obtaining character, in portrayals that were carefully planned and scripted by Miss Austen. *Life Lessons from Jane Austen's Pride and Prejudice* examines Jane's purposeful plan, searching out the depths of her memorable personalities, and seeking the profundity of her meaningful lessons in life, in morality, and in young love.

Fans of both the *Pride and Prejudice* novel and the movies who appreciated Miss Austen's strong moral values will appreciate this easy flowing study of her comedic characters and her Christian character, making a great love story even better.

Wifely Wisdom for Sometimes Foolish Husbands:
From Laura Ingalls and Almanzo to Abigail and Nabal

A Christian wife may be caught between a rock and a hard place. The rock is Christ, the spiritual rock who commands wives to be submissive to their husbands; and the hard place is the husband, who sometimes has less than perfect wisdom. *Wifely Wisdom for Sometimes Foolish Husbands* discusses the pickle of a wife being submissive but still sharing her wisdom with a husband during his few and far-between foolish moments. Such examples include Laura Ingalls sharing her insights with her husband Almanzo Wilder; Ma and Pa Ingalls; and Abigail and Nabal, whose very name meant fool.

This is a sprightly look at a serious subject, when marriage is under attack from all sides as never before. If a wife can share basic wisdom with her husband when he acts like Nabal, then they may save their marriage and rescue their family from destruction. Laura and Almanzo shared good times and bad times, through chucked churns and hot lid lifters, times when she spoke and times when she didn't, times when he listened and times when he didn't, and through all that their marriage lasted for sixty-three years. *Wifely Wisdom for Sometimes Foolish Husbands* may add a few years, or decades, or a lifetime, to your marriage.

Daring to Love like God:
Marriage as a Spiritual Union

The *Love Dare*© program, made famous in the movie *Fireproof*©, was for people whose marriages had problems, to dare them to take steps to better those marriages. *Daring to Love like God* is the next step, for people with good marriages, who are not about to split, who love God and each other, and who want to grow to become a true spiritual union.

This is one of the great miracles in creation: two people, with different abilities, personalities and wants, who become one, with each other and with God. If you want to be challenged to the very best marriage, *Daring to Love like God* leads you up that path.

76112913R00114

Made in the USA
Columbia, SC
29 August 2017